scribner

NEW YORK

LONDON

TORONTO

SYDNEY

TOKYO

SINGAPORE

DANIEL GORDIS

GOD

WAS

NOT

IN

THE

FIRE

———————◇———————

THE SEARCH FOR A SPIRITUAL JUDAISM

SCRIBNER
1230 AVENUE OF THE AMERICAS
NEW YORK, NY 10020

DESIGNED BY SONGHEE KIM
MANUFACTURED IN THE UNITED STATES OF AMERICA

1 3 5 7 9 10 8 6 4 2

LIBRARY OF CONGRESS CATALOGING-IN-PUBLICATION DATA
GORDIS, DANIEL.
GOD WAS NOT IN THE FIRE: THE SEARCH FOR A SPIRITUAL
JUDAISM / DANIEL GORDIS.
P.   CM.
INCLUDES BIBLIOGRAPHICAL REFERENCES AND INDEX.
1. JUDAISM. 2. SPIRITUAL LIFE—JUDAISM. 3. JEWISH WAY OF LIFE.
I. TITLE.
BM561.G67   1995
296—DC20   95-17867   CIP

ISBN 0-684-80390-9

FOR BETH

כי היא מקור הברכה

There was a great and mighty wind,
splitting mountains and shattering rocks
by the power of the Lord;
but the Lord was not in the wind.
After the wind—an earthquake;
but the Lord was not in the earthquake.
After the earthquake—fire;
but the Lord was not in the fire.
And after the fire—kol demamah dakkah,
the sound of delicate silence.

I KINGS 19

CONTENTS

ACKNOWLEDGMENTS

IN WRITING THIS BOOK I HAVE BEEN AIDED IMMEA-surably by the support and encouragement of a variety of friends and colleagues. It is a pleasure to acknowledge my debt to them all.

It has been almost a decade since I began working at the University of Judaism. During these years the university has been consistently supportive of my study, research, and writing. In particular, the university's president, Dr. Robert Wexler, has been much more than a valued colleague for many years. Almost since we met, Bob has been a loyal and devoted friend as well. It is no exaggeration to say that without his encouragement and support I could never have written this book. Dr. David Lieber, now the university's president emeritus, was president when I first came to the university. I am indebted to him for his invitation to join the faculty and administration, for all he did to enable me to complete my graduate study, and for the uniquely creative, nurturing, and challenging working and learning environment he created.

Mr. Francis Maas, chair of the board of directors, has been instrumental in making my work at the university as rewarding as it is. He has also offered insightful career advice at critical junctures. My family and I are proud to count the Maas family among our friends.

Two other colleagues at the university also provided critical assistance along the way. Mimi Sells read very early drafts of the first few chapters and deftly steered me away from what would have been devastating errors in tone and focus. David Wolpe offered consistent encouragement as the project unfolded and generously shared his expertise about the world of agents, publishers, and book writing in general.

Much of the material in this book was first developed for lectures that I delivered at the Brandeis-Bardin Institute in my role as dean of the Brandeis Collegiate Institute during the summers of 1990 through 1993. My debt to BCI knows no bounds. It was at BCI that I was first prompted to conceive a broad statement about the value of Jewish life, and the summers that I spent there afforded me a cadre of brilliant colleagues and talented students with whom to explore and hone these ideas. Brandeis-Bardin is a unique institution in the Jewish world, and the opportunity to be part of its faculty and staff for several years has been one of the great gifts of my professional and Jewish lives. To my colleagues during those summers and to the BCIers whose questions and ideas are woven throughout these pages, my deepest thanks.

Special thanks are due in particular to Dr. Alvin Mars, executive vice president of Brandeis-Bardin, who extended to me the invitation to join its faculty and, eventually, to serve as dean of BCI. Indeed, my debt to Alvin extends far beyond BCI. At each stage of my education and career, Alvin helped critical opportunities come my way. He offered me my first serious educational position at Camp Ramah, and then years later, when he was vice president for academic affairs at the

University of Judaism, he was instrumental in making it possible for me to work at UJ. In inviting me to join the Brandeis-Bardin community, Alvin continued his "tradition" of affording me crucial opportunities that would shape my thinking and work. This book is in many ways a product of the opportunities he afforded me, and no words seem adequate when I seek to express my appreciation for all he has meant to me.

Numerous other people contributed to this project in critical ways. Robert Bleiweiss, publisher and editor of the *Jewish Spectator*, invited me to serve as a senior contributing editor of the journal, and published several papers that were initial explorations of some of the ideas found throughout these chapters. I am grateful to Bob not only for his collegiality but for his friendship as well. Vida Bleiweiss and Ellen Anreder, other members of the *Spectator* team, gave me much to think about as these articles developed and first appeared in print.

Shawn and Tom Fields-Meyer, whom I first came to know when Shawn was my student at the University of Judaism, have since become treasured friends and trusted critics. Both of them read and carefully edited early drafts of the first several chapters of the book and helped to shape this book's tone and style. It was Tom who suggested that I contact his literary agent, Richard Pine, a suggestion that dramatically changed the course of this project. Mr. Richard Ziman, a generous and devoted friend of the University of Judaism, provided me with secluded office space during the summer of 1994, when most of this manuscript was written.

Richard Pine is a superb literary agent. He is also a profoundly thoughtful and sensitive human being, and I am deeply grateful that our paths crossed. He gently prodded me to keep at it when the going got somewhat tough, exuding a consistent confidence that this book could come to be. I look forward to working with him for many years. My colleagues at Scribner have been consistently helpful and insightful. My publisher, Susan Moldow, has been supportive of the project from the outset and has offered insightful advice throughout. I am deeply fortunate that Susan asked Jane Rosenman, executive editor at Scribner, to work on this manuscript with me. Jane's skills and judgment have improved this manuscript in ways too numerous to count. Linda Good, Jane's editorial assistant, has done a wonderful job of attending to the myriad details involved in this book's production.

I was profoundly blessed to grow up in a family deeply devoted to Jewish tradition and study. Though I have been fortunate to have many wonderful teachers, no one shaped my thinking about Jewish life more than my late grandfather, Rabbi Robert Gordis. Though I always miss him, I particularly wish that he had lived to see this book completed. The approach to Jewish life presented here is somewhat different from his, but I am certain that he would have seen throughout its pages the profound influence he had on me. That, more than anything, would have been the most appropriate way for me to express the thanks he so richly deserves.

My parents raised their three sons in a loving, supportive, and challenging home in which Jewish tradition was a given but in which we were also encouraged to think for ourselves. I can imagine no better combination. The mere fact that I decided to write this book is due in large measure to the values they inculcated in us.

I've dedicated this book to my wife, Beth. Beth is the person who has taught me more than anyone else about the importance of spirituality in Jewish life. Ever since we met half a lifetime ago, she has tempered my love for Judaism's intellectual tradition with an appreciation for its mystery, its beauty, and its warmth. Once I began work on this book, she was my most faithful supporter and toughest critic. She's read every word of this book more times than I believe she would care to recall, told me when entire chapters had to be rewritten or even discarded, and spent countless hours editing, polishing, and improving the text. I would never have thought of writing this book if not for her, and could never have completed it without her help. This book is in many ways her book.

Our children—Talia, Aviel, and Micha—have watched more or less patiently as their father spent entire months in front of the computer. Young as they are, I believe that they already have a deep sense of the power and beauty of Jewish life. I hope that as they grow older the commitments reflected in this book will become their commitments and that our passions for Jewish life will become their passions. That, more than anything else, would give Beth and me a sense of ultimate accomplishment.

JANUARY 1995
TU BI-SHEVAT 5755

A NOTE TO THE READER

◇

THE PAGES THAT FOLLOW CITE AND DISCUSS A WIDE variety of Jewish texts. Though some of the translations are exclusively mine, I have often been aided by existing works. The translations used have been taken from a variety of sources. For the Hebrew Bible, I have generally used the *Tanakh: The Holy Scriptures—the New JPS Translation According to the Traditional Hebrew Text* (Jewish Publication Society, 1985). Selections from the Christian Bible are based on the King James Version and the Jerusalem Bible (Doubleday, 1966). Selections from the Mishnah are based on translations by Jacob Neusner (Yale University Press, 1988) and the Soncino Talmud (Soncino Press, 1977). Selections from the Talmud and Midrash Rabbah are also based on the Soncino translations of those texts.

I have used a variety of translations for the liturgical texts discussed throughout this book. I have used mainly *Siddur Sim Shalom* (Rabbinical Assembly and United Synagogue of America, 1985) and *The Complete Artscroll Siddur* (Mesorah

Publications, Ltd., 1985). For the translation of *Adon Olam*, I used *The Hirsch Siddur* (Feldheim Publishers, 1969). The translation of the Seven Wedding Blessings is taken from *A Rabbi's Manual* (Rabbinical Assembly, 1965). Translations of Shabbat songs are based primarily on Robert Ives's *Shabbat and Festival Shiron* (Robert Ives, 1992).

I have rarely used any of these translations without modification. Almost all have been at least slightly revised either for clarity or to suit the specific context at hand. Transliterations of Hebrew and Aramaic words generally follow the style of the *Encyclopedia Judaica*. With words that are commonly used in everyday speech such as "chutzpah" and "mitzvah," more colloquial transliterations have been employed.

The three midrashic sources about God and the existence of evil were first collected in Chapter Three of Barry Holtz's *Back to the Sources* (Summit Books, 1984). Though my reading of those texts differs somewhat from the discussion presented there, I am indebted to that volume for suggesting the comparison. As I specifically note in Chapter Six, much of my reading of the weekday *Amidah* is based on the insightful work and teaching of Professor Reuven Kimmelman of Brandeis University.

Some of the material in this book is based on preliminary explorations of these ideas published elsewhere. These include several articles in the *Jewish Spectator*, among them "Jewish Love, Jewish Law: Can Liberal Judaism Weather the Intermarriage Crisis?" (Winter 1992); "Believing, Behaving, and Belonging: The Proverbial Cart and Horse Revisited" (Fall 1992); "Where Has All the Passion Gone? American Jews and Their Jewish Estrangement" (Spring 1993); and "Honey from the Word: Yeshiva Learning for Liberal Jews?" (Winter 1994). Some of the ideas in Chapter Five were also preliminarily explored in "The End of Survivalist Judaism? American Jews in Search of Direction" in *Sh'ma: A Journal of Jewish Responsibility* (Vol. 24, no. 466, 21 January 1994).

INTRODUCTION

◇

THE CRISIS AND THE OPPORTUNITY

IN 1985, THE SOCIOLOGIST AND EDUCATOR CHARLES
Silberman published *A Certain People*, a study of Jews in America. He argued that anti-Jewish sentiment in the United States
was then at an all-time low, and that Jews were more secure in
this country than they ever had been before. "We are, in fact,"
Silberman suggested, "in the early stages of a major revitalization of Jewish religious, intellectual and cultural life—one that
is likely to transform and strengthen American Judaism."* But
just five years later, the National Council of Jewish Federations released its *1990 National Jewish Population Study*, a demographic portrait of American Jews that indicated that Jews
were abandoning Judaism at an unprecedented rate. These
findings provoked Jews of all stripes to speak openly of a crisis
in the American Jewish community. "Continuity" has become

---

*Charles C. Silberman, *A Certain People: American Jews and Their Lives
Today* (New York: Summit Books, 1985), p. 25.

a virtual mantra. Many Jews have grown convinced that the very survival of American Judaism is now in question.

There is an irony in this latest Jewish crisis; it is the result of a long-standing Jewish dream finally coming true. For centuries, Jews longed to live in a society in which we would be seen as ordinary human beings. We wanted to succeed—or to fail—on our own merits, not because we were Jewish. We dreamed of tolerance, of understanding, of the mere possibility that we could *choose* to be Jews. We reveled in the fantasy of a world in which no one would brand us as Jews, a world in which we would consciously embrace our community out of a desire to be a part of it. We wanted the option to *decide* to adopt Jewish life, not to have it forced upon us or forcibly taken from us.

That dream has finally come true. In America, Jews have found a community that accepts us. The great universities of North America have Jewish enrollments far outweighing the proportion of Jews in the population, and almost all professions and neighborhoods are open to Jews. Being Jewish no longer means always having to feel like the "other" or "the outsider."

Of course, anti-Jewish sentiment has not completely abated, and Jews have cause for continuing vigilance. But those vestiges of times largely gone by ought not distract us from enormous changes in the Jewish condition. Secular society no longer brands us as Jews; for modern Jews, Judaism is a choice. Silberman was right; contemporary America is more accepting of Jews than any other culture has been.

But Silberman was also wrong. While he was correct about how the non-Jewish world's attitudes to Jews were changing, he was mistaken about what that would mean for the Jewish future. He failed to appreciate the challenge that Jewish freedom would present. Without non-Jews to force Jews into Judaism, many Jews now are not sure how to answer the question "Why be Jewish?"

While Jews can choose Judaism, they can also choose to be part of something else, or of nothing. Today, Jews are free to leave the Jewish community without joining any other religious community. This is a uniquely modern phenomenon. In the past, even when Jews could leave the Jewish world, they usually had to join some other faith community. (In Europe, for example, they often had to convert to Christianity.) But today, the widespread social acceptance of Jews and the pervasive secularism of North America and even Israel mean that Jews need not convert out of Judaism; they can simply drop out.

Modern Jews—sophisticated and educated to unprecedented degrees—now find that they need good reasons to identify as Jews. A Jewish way of life is no longer the natural choice. The closely knit Jewish communities of generations gone by, the palpably Jewish neighborhoods of yesteryear, have disappeared. The striking ethnicity of an earlier Jewish life— the European accents, a quaint amazement at American life, and virtually complete comfort with Jewish customs and tradition—has largely dissipated. Even nostalgia is running low; young Jews today do not have their parents' and grandparents' visceral associations with the pungent smells of chicken in the oven before Shabbat or of the peaceful moments associated with the lighting of Friday night's candles. Neighborhoods, ethnicity, nostalgia—powerful motivators a generation ago, they are but memories today. Now, Jews must consciously decide whether and how to identify as Jews.

These new options have made Jews more circumspect than we were previously. The questions we ask and that we consider so vital were rare only a generation ago: What does it mean to be a Jew? What does the Jewish people stand for? Do we have "an obligation" to remain part of the Jewish people? Where does that obligation come from? Is it authentic? Who (or what) makes that obligation real? Would our lives be significantly impoverished if we chose not to make Jewish connection a central part of life?

To be sure, not everyone asks these questions. On one end of the spectrum are Jewish secularists, who consider religious life antiquated or irrelevant and who need no justification for abandoning it. At the other extreme are the committed Jews, to whom these issues seem trivial. For them, being Jewish and living a Jewish life is not a matter of decision making; it is simply part of how they were raised and a natural outgrowth of their belief systems. To live their lives in any other way would be as unthinkable as moving to a country where they did not speak the language and had no hopes of learning it. For these Jews, to wonder why they are Jewish would be like wondering why they love the people they do. What matters is that they love them—and that they live their lives as expressions of that commitment.

But there are many Jews for whom such questions are neither irrelevant nor trivial. For many modern Jews, these questions give expression to the very crux of their conflicts regarding Jewish involvement. "Why be Jewish?" "If I choose not to be Jewish, what do I lose?" And perhaps even more fundamentally, they ask: "What does Jewish life mean? What does Judaism offer that I cannot find in secular society?"

Why are so many Jews simply opting out of Jewish life? It is not merely because of society's openness, but rather because for many the old ties to Jewish life have eroded, and most Jews have no plausible explanation to justify trying to preserve them. Modern Jewish communities have failed to tailor a message about Judaism's meaning for bright, educated, and sophisticated Jews. To those Jews, therefore, Judaism seems outmoded, confining, and—often—utterly incomprehensible.

There are a wide variety of additional explanations for Jews' flight from Jewish life. For some, the causes are economic or demographic; Jewish life can be costly, and some Jews live in places in which there are virtually no Jewish communities to join. For others, the primary considerations are theoretical issues of theology or morality; to their minds, the pervasiveness of human suffering and tragedy makes it difficult to justify *any* religious commitments. But for many Jews, the causes are much simpler: Jewish life has never seemed worthy of much attention or commitment. Many of the Jews who choose to leave Jewish life—or who elect to make Judaism more peripheral than their parents or grandparents did—do so primarily because Jewish life has never spoken to them in a serious way. Unless modern Jews begin to see Jewish life as intellectually satisfying and spiritually enriching, they will not come back.

It would be unreasonable to hope to alter profoundly such a widespread trend with a single book. And this book has no such expectations. My simple goal is to portray Jewish life and its meaning in a way radically different from most contemporary Jewish educational approaches. The message: Jewish life merits the attention of modern Jews not by virtue of the call of nostalgia or because of an amorphous sense of obligation, but by virtue of its potential role in our lives as a compelling, meaningful, and enriching enterprise that helps define precisely who and what we are.

The following chapters will examine at least part of the Jewish experience through a new prism. For those people to whom the Jewish tradition has never spoken, I hope that this volume may portray Jewish life as far more meaningful or spiritually enriching than it has seemed in the past. For those Jews for whom Jewish life is part of the regular rhythm of life, I hope that this book may cast a new and stimulating light upon that which is already familiar. For people wondering what it is that others have found so attractive about Jewish life, I hope that this book will provide a sense of how Judaism offers a unique approach to seeking an intellectually and spiritually compelling way of life. For Jews to whom Judaism has always seemed "home" (even if a sometimes uncomfortable one), I hope that this volume will help articulate why Jewish life sometimes seems so core to who we are.

There is much about Jewish life that this book will not address. No single book can address all of Jewish tradition. The elements of Jewish life discussed in the following chapters, however, are those elements that are central to Judaism's providing the compelling, richly textured, and meaningful spiritual experience many Jews are seeking and that Judaism can have the capacity to provide today as it has in the past. Jews interested in spirituality and in a religion that will touch the very fiber of their beings do not have to turn elsewhere to find it. Nor must they radically reconfigure Judaism. They simply need an opportunity to learn how Jewish tradition addresses these eternal needs. This book is designed to afford such an opportunity.

At the opening of this section, I mentioned the sense of "crisis" in modern Jewish life. "Crisis" in Hebrew is *mash-ber'*, a word also used for birthstool, a seat upon which a woman in ancient times sat as she gave birth. The Hebrew language recognized that while crises are often frightening, they are also filled with potential. Adversity, our tradition suggests, needs to be turned into opportunity.

The state of Judaism in the modern world leads to precisely such an opportunity. The choice of many modern Jews not to commit substantially to Jewish life does, indeed, pose a serious challenge to Judaism and to Jewish communities throughout the world. But it also presents modern Jewish communities with a valuable opportunity—the opportunity to examine the ways in which Jewish life is communicated and transmitted, and to express more clearly the powerful spiritual and emotional components of Jewish life. The Jewish community needs to earn the allegiance of its people. Modernity offers us the chance.

JUDAISM
AS A
SPIRITUAL
ODYSSEY

WE ALL WRESTLE. ALL HUMAN BEINGS—IN ALL AGES AND of all generations—struggle with similar questions: What deserves our love, and what should we hate? What should we pursue in the relatively few years we are alive, and what should we shun? What is ultimately valuable, and how do we seek it? What is ultimately devoid of value, and how can we avoid it? How do we need to live, to feel, or to dream if we are to make our lives worth something? Jews add another question to the list: Does Judaism have anything relevant to say about these issues anymore?

Many Jews are not certain how to answer that question. It has been years since anything Jewish touched them profoundly. Because they are hesitant to commit to something they do not fully understand, the early part of their adult lives unfolds without giving much attention to their Jewish roots. As they leave home, they find themselves preoccupied with college, a career, marriage, and a family. In the midst of all that, Jewish commitments can seem not to fit. Life proceeds apace, often without our giving Judaism much thought.

Much of the time, however, it is one poignant moment that tends to reawaken our struggle with Jewish life. That moment is the birth of a child. In Jewish life, the arrival of a child—and particularly the arrival of a son—brings with it a whole set of Jewish expectations about the performance of an age-old ritual, the *bris* (a ritual circumcision).

For many Jewish parents, the moment of preparing for a *bris* proves highly ironic and discomfiting. For while they are not particularly religious, they are insistent that their son simply needs to have a *bris*. In some cases, even though they do not know a tremendous amount about Judaism, they sense that this is something that simply must happen. Suddenly, these new parents feel that they do not want to be the ones to "break" the centuries-long chain of Jewish tradition. A desire for Jewish connection, latent for many years, now overwhelms them.

But at the same time, contemplating a *bris* can also be deeply unsettling. For among the many reasons that Jews often find Judaism so difficult is their sense that Jewish life is often too mysterious, even irrational. Nothing evokes that sense more than a *bris*. Why, parents wonder, should they do something so primal, so seemingly irrational and possibly even cruel to their newborn child? Why should they insist on this primitive rite, one of the seemingly least appealing facets of a tradition from which they have long felt estranged?

Ultimately, the question about a *bris* becomes a question about Judaism. "Why have a *bris*?" really asks a deeper question, one that many modern Jews struggle to answer. That question is simply "Why be Jewish?"

WHY JEWISH LIFE?

That question is much more complicated and difficult than it might seem. Most modern Jews can probably not explain even to themselves why they feel whatever connection they do to the Jewish people, and why they choose to participate in Jewish rituals from time to time.

What honest response can they offer? They cannot say to their spouses, or to themselves, that they want a *bris*—or some other form of Jewish expression—solely because that is what Jewish tradition requires. There are a myriad of other things Jewish tradition requires that they ignore, usually without guilt. They also cannot claim that they believe that engaging in this ceremony will be particularly meaningful for them, because they well know that their experiences with Jewish ritual have often felt empty, foreign, and forbidding. For years, they have dutifully attended synagogue services at crucial moments in the Jewish year, but they have never had the sense that God hears them or answers them. Passover Seders, theoretically about the rich topic of freedom and redemption, never seemed to address any issues that truly matter.

Many Jews today may say they believe Jewish life should or must continue, or that they do not want to be the ones to "break the chain." But those responses simply defer another question: Why? Why should Jewish life continue? Not many Jews, committed or not, can offer a coherent response to that fundamental question.

To questions this profound, good answers prove elusive. Unfortunately, we often hear answers that do more damage than good, turning Jews away from Jewish life rather than drawing them near.

THE ARGUMENTS THAT WILL NOT WORK

When we ask the question "Why be Jewish?" we confront crucial questions of personal identity. Answers that touch us must say something about the deeply personal issues that trouble and motivate us, or ultimately they will do nothing to make Jewish life worthwhile. Modern Jews want explanations of Jewish life that touch their humanity; most of what we hear, however, falls far short of that. Let's consider three of the most common—and most flawed—arguments.

AVENGING THE SHOAH

Many of us have heard people argue that Jews have obligations to perpetuate Judaism because of the *Shoah* (the Hebrew word for the Holocaust)—that is, so as not to give Hitler a posthumous victory.* "So many Jews died for being Jewish," the argument runs, "that *we*, who live much more privileged lives, have no right to sell them out."

But most modern Jews have learned a very different lesson from those tragic events. They focus not only on the obvious German attempt to eradicate the Jewish people, but on the complicity of the educated and supposedly refined Western world in the murder of millions of innocent Jewish and non-Jewish men, women, and children. Many modern Jews, educated in a multicultural and open society, take from the *Shoah* a determination to prevent future genocides. For better or worse, they believe that the lessons from Nazi Germany have more to do with flawed human nature and people's capacity for evil than they do with the survival of one particular group.

**Shoah, in Hebrew, means "calamity." "Holocaust" is an English word that means "burnt offering" or "sacrifice to God." The Jews of Europe in the 1930s and 1940s were not sacrificed—they were murdered. There is a tremendous difference; this book uses the word *Shoah* in order to take that difference seriously.

Therefore, when we invoke the memories of Hitler's victims in order to convince another generation of Jews to remain Jewish, we inevitably fail. Modern Jews will make Judaism a part of their lives if it is relevant and meaningful, not because of a war fought and concluded long before they were born. Either Judaism will speak to their souls and their hearts, or they will stop listening.

ETHNIC SUPERIORITY

Another flawed argument for Jewish continuity is based on not-so-subtle claims of Jewish intellectual or ethical superiority. Proponents of this argument suggest (though hesitantly, for they know that Jews are still a small and sometimes vulnerable minority) that Jews generally reflect a higher standard of morality in their daily lives than non-Jews. Though the failings of several prominent and committed Jews on Wall Street make such arguments somewhat difficult to defend, one can still hear them expressed often.

But suggestions of superiority—intellectual, ethical, or otherwise—offend many modern Jews. This country has afforded Jews virtually complete exposure to the Western and secular worlds. Jews have learned and observed that the non-Jewish society around them is richly populated with bright, sensitive, and ethically serious individuals, whose moral sensibilities are no less informed by their Christian (or other) heritage than ours are by Judaism.

It is also certainly true that Jewish life has always placed a premium on devotion to study and ethical behavior. But does Jewish tradition really shape the fundamental outlook of most modern Jews? To what extent do these traditional values of study, particularly of complex and difficult classical Jewish texts, imbue the lives of most modern Jews? Ultimately, despite a generally good historical record in the realm of ethical behavior, most Jews today do not believe that Jews are more intelligent or ethical than their non-Jewish counterparts.

Thus, rather than draw these Jews nearer to Jewish life, arguments such as these tend to push them away.

PRESERVING THE CHAIN

Yet another flawed claim about the importance of Jewish continuity is based on the notion of continuity for continuity's sake. This argument appears in several forms. One version argues that if Jews do not identify with their community, Jews will disappear! But this circular reasoning does not explain why that disappearance would be a problem. Another version of the argument suggests that Judaism has represented the value of continuity in life; it insists that there is value in certain things remaining constant from generation to generation, particularly in our rapidly changing world. Jews should participate in Jewish life, this argument claims, because ancient traditions have intrinsic value, and we should preserve them.

But these claims prove no more effective than either of the previous two arguments. When an adult in her or his thirties, keenly aware of advancing age and deeply interested in beginning a family, struggles with whether or not to become romantically involved with someone who is not Jewish, history or communal survival do not seem important. Theoretical discussions of continuity seem much less pressing than other more personal and primal considerations.

There is yet another problem with the argument of continuity for its own sake. Often, people are proudest of the changes they have made during the courses of their lives. For some, the important change can be personal, as in escaping a harmful family pattern of noncommunication or emotional indifference. Others derive a deep sense of accomplishment and satisfaction from working for change in the public arena. Whether in race relations, treatment of the poor, or even making changes in certain elements of Jewish tradition, they see change as valuable and laudable. For them, continuity for its own sake is not only irrelevant, it is often even pernicious.

Continuity alone, therefore, will certainly not provide them a reason to remain Jewish.

And the argument has other weaknesses. Very often, the advocates of Jewish continuity for the sake of continuity live Jewish lives wholly unlike the Jewish lives their grandparents lived. Often, their ancestors were much more observant or Jewishly knowledgeable than they are, but these Jewish advocates still claim to represent the ideal of not breaking the chain. Similarly, some of these advocates of continuity advocate new and more equal roles for women, even though that is not what Jews have always done.

Finally, continuity is not an absolute. Even those Jews who are deeply committed to Jewish tradition often favor some changes in Jewish life. Perhaps we favor increased tolerance and respect of non-Jews. Perhaps we are committed to affording girls and women more opportunities for serious Jewish study. For some Jews, Judaism's values regarding sexuality seem outdated. Perhaps it is some other change that we urge. Regardless of the specific issue, however, continuity is an absolute for very few of us. Who should determine what should and should not remain constant? Who is to say that someone's choice of a radically less intensive way of Jewish life is wrong?

Each of these arguments for Jewish continuity is deeply flawed. And beyond their individual weaknesses, these failed responses share two additional flaws: First, none of them addresses the majestic breadth and sophistication of Jewish tradition. None of the responses reviewed here does anything to explain why traditional Jews study a body of sacred texts, pray three times a day, eat only kosher food, or wear a *kippah* (yarmulkah). None of these arguments explains how any of these practices contributed to the spiritual fulfillment of Jewish life generations ago.

Perhaps more importantly, none of these answers explains
how Judaism can enrich our own lives. Ultimately, what we all
want is to live lives that matter. Deep in our souls, we desperately want to live the kind of life that we could look back upon
with pride and with deep satisfaction. But what would such a
life look like? Is there anything we can do in our modern world
to work toward that sense of satisfaction, that feeling of contentment? Does Judaism play some role in that quest? None of
the answers discussed above speaks to how Judaism might help
us on that journey.

Unless explanations of the Jewish tradition and arguments
for its relevance address these questions, nothing anyone says
will make a difference. Ultimately, modern Jews need a substantive reason not to break the chain. Any answer to the
question "Why remain Jewish?" has to address more than one
small element of the wide spectrum of Jewish expression. It
must speak of Judaism in the broadest of terms; our answer to
"Why be Jewish?" has to convince us that commitment to Jewish life will revive our spirit, rekindle our passion for living,
and infuse our lives with joy and with meaning.

JEWISH LIFE AND OUR "ULTIMATE" QUESTIONS

If we are so disenchanted and alienated, why is it still so difficult to walk away from Jewish life? Why do Jewish adults, who
often feel only marginally Jewish, still wrestle with giving up a
piece of their lives that they never fully enjoyed or appreci-
ated? Why are parents of college students—often only marginally connected to Judaism themselves—so concerned that
their children will move away from Jewish life during those
first crucial years of independence?

When parents who are scarcely involved with Jewish life
learn that their daughter or son plans to marry a non-Jewish

person, why are they so often distraught? And why do their children, even as they resist their parents' intervention in what seems a deeply personal decision, sometimes sense an obligation to take this Jewish issue seriously? Why do so many of us still feel such ambivalence about leaving Jewish life?

For many Jews, even Jews who have tired of the empty, unfulfilled emotions they associate with religion in general and Jewish life in particular, it is difficult to walk away because they sense that what they are tempted to walk away from is not the best that Judaism has to offer. They persist and linger in Jewish life because they deeply suspect that something has been missing from their Judaism, that the Jewish lives they have lived have not been the "real thing." Jewish life, they feel, could be more passionate and emotional than it has been for them. They realize that, although their own Jewish experiences may have been intellectually stultifying, aesthetically unpleasant, or emotionally forbidding, for other people Jewish experience is different, better, satisfying, meaningful. They may nostalgically recall their grandparents or great-grandparents, whose Jewish lives might well have been rich with meaning and power. They may have friends for whom traditional Jewish communities offer a profound sense of belonging, community, and nurturing. They may read the testimonies of other Jews who speak of "rediscovering" their Jewish roots and the ways in which that rediscovery brought a sense of peace and spirituality into their lives.

And they question why that has never happened for them. Where, they wonder, did all the passion go? How did we and our Jewishness become so estranged?

Ironically, we refuse to let go of Jewish life not because Jewish life has been satisfying, but because even though it has let us down, we deeply suspect that it has more to offer. Judaism promises a sense of belonging to a rich history; we may not feel it, but we would like to. We are taught that Judaism has a unique system of ethics with profound insights; we may not yet know what those insights are, but we are interested, and are hesitant to abandon such a tradition. For these reasons and others, we conclude that the chain must not be broken; perhaps Jewish life could "work," if not for us, then for the next generation.

But what would it mean for Jewish life to "work"? What would Jewish life have to "become" in order for generations of modern, questing, and sophisticated Jews to take it seriously? What would Jewish life have to offer for intermarriage rates to decline, for rates of communal affiliation to rise? What is it that a relatively comfortable and affluent modern Jewish community on the eve of the twenty-first century really needs that a two-thousand-year-old religious tradition could provide?

What we know from the phenomenon of professionally and socially upwardly mobile young Jews returning to Judaism (a movement commonly called the *ba'al teshuvah* movement, or the "returnees") is that beyond all the trappings of success and comfort, young people—like all people—seek a sense of meaning for their lives. They, like deeply religious people, are consumed by the question of what their lives ultimately mean, how their lives can be most richly lived, what they would like to leave behind in the world. More than anything, they desperately wish to believe that they matter. And more often than not, their deepest trauma stems from not being entirely certain that they do.

For us to take Jewish life seriously, Judaism must speak to these questions. Judaism, Jewish institutions, Jewish leaders, and Jewish books must successfully convey the impression that Judaism is not about the rote mastery of ancient texts, about restrictions on our behavior and autonomy, and about outmoded concepts of right and wrong. It must transmit the sense that Jewish life is about ultimacy. We will have to be convinced that Judaism—at its most basic but also at its most profound—speaks to the fundamental questions that haunt and inspire all human beings.

The great irony, however, is that Judaism never stopped speaking to these questions. Modern Jews simply stopped listening. Eager to fit into a society that seemed more welcoming than any that Jews had ever experienced, North American Jews spent the 1950s, 1960s, and 1970s creating suburban Jewish life as an American ethnicity, seeking to remain distinct enough to survive, but similar enough to other American ethnicities for Jews not to seem overtly different from their non-Jewish neighbors.

We minimized the importance of Hebrew, forgetting that the poetry of any culture when translated must inevitably lose some of its power. We avoided speaking in terms that said "Judaism requires . . . ," forgetting that all dimensions of our lives that truly matter ultimately make demands on us.

In the process of making this transition, we stripped Jewish life of the overtly religious trappings that made it appear *too* different. We found it more comfortable to speak of Jewish life in terms of a moral struggle for social action than as a process of living life in dialogue with a series of sacred texts. We preferred a sanitized religious experience, emulating the aesthetics of liberal American churches, to the seemingly disorganized and cacophonous sounds of the traditional *shtibl* (informal synagogue). And we pressed our rabbis to re-create themselves in what we perceived as the model of America's tamed and (relative to our previous rabbis) inconspicuous Protestant ministers. All of these steps made Judaism seem less strange, less foreign, and less un-American. They also made Judaism *less.*

A UNIQUE CONTENT FOR JEWISH LIFE?

Therein lies the problem. Ultimately, Jewish life for many Jews seems no richer than an embodiment of their liberal values with a slight Jewish flavor; Jewish life in American suburbia does nothing substantive to answer the questions that consume sleepless nights. For many modern Jews, Jewish tradition simply seems to communicate the values derived from politicians, interest groups, books, journals, friends, spouses, and others in an identifiably Jewish language. The medium may be unique, but the message seems commonplace or even trivial. Why, Jews commonly wonder, do they need to go to a synagogue if the message is identical to what they hear in the media and throughout the rest of society? Can't Judaism say something that Jews will not hear from other realms of society?

But in fairness, we cannot lay the blame for a seemingly commonplace message fully at the feet of the Jewish tradition. For how could we expect Jewish life to address the truly fundamental questions surrounding our humanity when we have robbed it of its religious and spiritual tools? American Jews are disappointed by Judaism because there is an ethical vocabulary, a rich tradition of practice, a liturgy filled with poetry, and much more that we no longer make part of our lives. We imagined that we could strip Jewish life of what uniquely qualified it to address our spiritual yearnings—and then expect it to touch our souls.

This trend became particularly pronounced when modern American academic and intellectual circles began to open their doors to Jewish students in unprecedented numbers. In the 1930s and 1940s, American Jewish leaders suddenly feared that the religious tradition of American Jews would seem hopelessly unsophisticated and primitive to those Jews who got a glimpse of academe. These leaders feared that as Jews became more exposed to the world of American higher education, they would find Judaism unacceptably nonrational, perhaps even primitive. Therefore, scholars like Rabbi Mordecai Kaplan (1881–1983) and others sought to "reconstruct" Jewish life so that it could compete even among a newly Western educated class of American Jews. Kaplan denied the idea of a supernatural God, dismissed the concept of a "chosen people," spoke of Jewish practices as being optional "folkways" rather than required rituals, and in general, sought to bring Judaism in line with what he saw as the American predilection for rationality. While Kaplan's program (ultimately called Reconstructionist Judaism) succeeded in many ways, the highly intellectualized product of his work failed to speak to the hearts of Jews. Reconstructionism, like other forms of American Jewish life, took on a highly respectable intellectual veneer, but many Jews suddenly felt—often without articulating this to themselves—that Judaism had become sterile. We might have been more comfortable speaking of the Torah as a collection of Jewish myths than as a sacred text, but American Jews suddenly had difficulty explaining why *their* myths mattered to them more than anyone else's. It might seem less intellectually problematic to speak of God as the "power that makes for salvation"—as Kaplan does—than as a supernatural being, but then what is left for those Jews who, like many other human beings, suddenly and at pivotal moments in their lives desperately want to feel the presence of the God their intellects forced them to abandon?

There *is* something less strange and mysterious about the highly choreographed service of the modern American Reform or Conservative service, but there is also something much less passionate about it. Early in this century, the great German-Jewish theologian, Franz Rosenzweig (1886–1929), happened upon a traditional synagogue on his way to convert to Christianity, and was forever transformed. Something about the power of the service he witnessed convinced him not to abandon Jewish tradition. Was it the mass of men identically clad in black and white prayer shawls, swaying en masse as they confronted their individual and collective failings? Was it the haunting melody of the *Kol Nidrei* prayer, recited only on the eve of Yom Kippur? Was it the power and mystery of prayer in the original Hebrew, which no other language fully captures? Or was it the experience of being enveloped by a traditional community from which all modern life, at least momentarily, seemed to be shut out? As a result of that experience, Rosenzweig remained Jewish, and subsequently became one of the century's great Jewish thinkers. Would the same have happened had he stepped into a typical modern American service? Would he have felt that power? Would he have sensed the intensity of passionate dialogue with God? Would the experience have been powerful enough to change his life? Is it powerful enough to influence ours?

American Jews have sought to sanitize Jewish ritual, for traditional ritual seems mysterious, inexplicable, nonrational. We sense something unsophisticated, almost embarrassing, about untempered ritual. As members of a culture that prides itself on intellectual prowess and scientific progress, we have found it difficult to take seriously a body of ritual that seems so very irrational. Why, we often ask derisively, should an allegedly modern tradition like Judaism regulate what we eat, apparently without rational motivations? Why do some Jewish communities continue to place restrictions on whom we can marry? How can we respect a tradition that expects women to immerse themselves in a ritual bath (*mikveh*) after each menstrual cycle?

These are serious challenges to Jewish tradition. But we are also more complicated and less rational beings than we often want to admit. There are moments in our lives when we desperately wish to be moved, when we submit to ritual willingly. Sometimes, those rituals are not Jewish—dinner at a favorite restaurant, an afternoon at the ballpark, an evening at the symphony, or a sunset walk along the beach. But often, we do choose Jewish ritual, even if that choice violates the intellectual commitments we believe we have made.

Even the most nontraditional Jews often want substantive elements of Jewish ritual at their weddings. When we get married, we want to feel something that words simply cannot express. There is something about the continuity of life and hope for a future that a *ḥuppah*—the traditional Jewish wedding canopy—expresses for them in ways that nothing else can. So even nonreligious Jews, who have long rebelled against the dictates of Jewish tradition, find a rabbi, rent a *ḥuppah*, and relish the rituals their intellects cannot justify.

And for many completely disaffected Jews, the words of the mourners' *Kaddish* prove starkly comforting at moments of loss. Many Jews do not understand the words of the *Kaddish* or the service in which it appears. If pressed, they would even admit that they are intellectually uncomfortable with the entire enterprise of prayer. So why does the *Kaddish* comfort them? Why do many previously nonconnected Jews find themselves coming back to synagogues to say *Kaddish* as part of a service to a God in whom they do not believe, in a tradition they feel is outdated or irrelevant? Why do we return to ritual even when our minds rebel against it?

We return because we want to feel. While the American Jewish edifices in which many Jews grew up allowed them to *think* about Jewish issues, they later discovered that they could think without the synagogue, the rabbi, the Jewish Center, or even their tradition. They could think on campus with their peers and colleagues or in the privacy of their homes in the company of a thought-provoking book. But Western culture and our newly diluted Judaism never satisfied our need to feel, to touch the transcendent in the world. So many of us, when we want to express that which goes beyond the mind and beyond reason, hark back to tradition out of our sense that maybe, if we are fortunate, returning to tradition will allow us to feel.

JUDAISM AND OUR TRANSCENDENT YEARNINGS

That is why today's young Jewish parents still want a *bris* for their sons. They want a *bris* because having a child is about the

most primal and transcendent parts of our humanity. Jews today still want to express that. It is not the Jewish chain linking
the past to the future that they do not want to sever. It is their
own chain, their link to a place in the world in which words
are subordinate to feelings, in which the ephemeral gives way
to the permanent, and in which the petty is finally overshad-
owed by the transcendent. They come to understand that the
reason for connecting to tradition is that Jewish life, for Jews
who understand it and are willing to invest in it, is the most
powerful way we know of expressing humanity.

Can Jewish life serve that function in our lives? Is that what
Jewish life is about? What do these all-encompassing questions
have to do with the holidays we may or may not have learned
about as children, or with the names of classical texts that we
never entirely understood or enjoyed? What does a tradition
that always seemed to focus more on being different and apart
have to do with the search for meaning in modern lives? How
is Jewish life about the modern search for meaning? Is our notion of Judaism as a search for transcendent meaning simply an
unjustified modern "spin" on an ancient tradition that actually
has nothing to do with these modern questions?

JEWISH LIFE AS AN ODYSSEY

The idea of a "spiritual odyssey" is not a new view of Judaism,
but rather, has long been the essence of Jewish life. Regardless
of what one believes about the origins of the Torah (an issue
to which I will return), the Bible is undeniably the most central document that Jews have read for thousands of years. It is
the virtual definition of their origins, their mission, and their
sense of who they are.

The Torah, a word that Jews use for the Five Books of
Moses, the first part of the Bible, is in many respects the "diary" of the Jewish people. Were any of us to find the diary of

our great-great-grandparents, we would not only save it but would savor it. We would read it carefully and repeatedly for what it could tell us about the places and people from which we come. Why? We would relish that diary because as we uncover our past, we discover parts of ourselves. We come to understand better the shadows and images that seem to pervade our parents, our siblings, our own psyches. We learn that no matter how hard we struggle to become unique, there are ways in which we are chillingly similar to those who came before us. In learning about our ancestors, we learn about ourselves.

What do we learn from this other "diary," the Torah that tells our story? We learn, among much else, that names are important. Biblical characters choose names for themselves and their children with care. Of particular importance are not only the names of individuals, but the name of the people now called "Jews."

As Moses and his followers leave Egypt and wander for forty years on their way to the Promised Land, the Torah calls them not Jews but the Children of Israel. Why Children of Israel? Israel, the second name of Jacob, seems an unlikely name for our people. Jacob is, after all, certainly not the best known of the patriarchs. Nor is he among the most heroic images in the Torah. Why not, then, the Children of Abraham? The Children of Isaac? Or even the Children of Moses, the man who secured Israelite freedom from Pharaoh and devoted his life to leading his people across the barren desert to a land he was never privileged to enter? Why would the tradition elect to call Jews "the Children of Israel"?

According to the Torah, God changes Jacob's name to Israel after Jacob flees from his brother Esau, who he believed wished to kill him. The Torah continues:

> That same night he arose, and taking his two wives, his two maidservants and his eleven children, he crossed the ford of the Jabbok [river]. . . . Jacob was left alone. And a

man wrestled with him until the break of dawn. When he saw that he had not prevailed against him, he wrenched Jacob's hip at its socket, so that the socket of his hip was strained as he wrestled with him. Then he said, "Let me go, for dawn is breaking." But he answered, "I will not let you go, unless you bless me." Said the other, "What is your name?" He replied, "Jacob." Said he, "Your name shall no longer be Jacob, but Israel, for you have wrestled with God and men and have prevailed."

(GENESIS 32:23–29)

The word "Israel," from the Hebrew *yisrael*, means "to struggle with God." How important is the Torah's selection of the Jewish people's name? Of all the many colorful and rich personalities described in the Torah, the tradition named this people after the one who wrestled with God. The Torah did not name us the Children of Abraham, which might have been taken as a reference to Abraham's willingness to sacrifice Isaac upon God's demand. Nor did the Torah see fit to name the Jews after Isaac, the meek, accommodating, and forgiving son who was bound on the altar and who throughout the rest of his life seemed the very embodiment of submission. Rather, the Torah saw fit to refer to the Jewish people as those descended from Israel, the one who wrestled with God.

The tradition suggests that to be the true descendants— children—of Israel, modern Jews should not assume that Jewish tradition demands only meek, submissive obedience. Jews are named for an ancestor who wrestled with God while on a journey—a suggestion that our tradition wants from us something much more complicated than mere subservience. Struggle and journey, after all, are what "odyssey" means.

We see the importance of struggle in Jewish life once again in the Torah's description of how the Jewish people moved from Egyptian slavery to life in the Promised Land. The geographic distances between the Nile and the Land of Canaan (modern-day Israel) are not great. Even a nomadic people could have traversed the distance in much less than the forty years that it took the Children of Israel to travel from Egypt to Canaan. Why this central role for the lengthy odyssey in Jewish tradition?

Once more, the value is in the struggle, in the process of forging a life filled with meaning. Perhaps the Torah and Jewish tradition are trying to suggest that the move from slavery to the Promised Land, just like the process of evolving in our own lives, never happens in a direct, linear progression. If religious life is about confronting life's most profound questions, we have no reason to expect it to be easy. If one of the elements that religious commitment ultimately injects into our lives is a series of ponderous reflections on the kinds of people that we wish to become and the ways in which to become such people, it will necessarily cause us to embark on difficult odysseys. Profound transformations, like the passage from slavery to freedom, are not easy. They demand wandering, the investment of time, and even difficult moments along the way.

If we imagine religious life as neatly packaged, perennial bliss, we trivialize the religious enterprise in general and Judaism in particular. None of our substantive relationships or our important commitments in life come easily. Nothing in our life that provides deep satisfaction comes without real work and struggle. Why should our religious life be any different?

Real Jewish life is a life of passionate struggle and honest searching. The Torah's clearest indication of this is that the story of the Jewish people both begins and concludes outside the Promised Land. God's very first words to Abram, the first Jew, are a command to begin an odyssey:

> The Lord spoke to Abram, "Go forth from your native land and from your father's house to the land that I will show you. I will make of you a great nation, and I will

bless you; I will make your name great, and you shall be a
blessing. . . ."

(GENESIS 12:1–2)

Thus, the very first words God utters to the very first Jew are
lekh-lekha—get up and move. Abram—as he was known before
God changed his name to Abraham—begins life outside the
Promised Land. Before anything else transpires between him
and God, God communicates the most important message of
all: Abram's life as a Jew—and therefore ours as well—needs to
be a gradual journey toward the Promised Land.

But that journey will not be easy—not for Abram, not for
us. God tells Abram to leave his homeland and the land of his
fathers, the land in which he is comfortable and where he may
feel he belongs, and to go to a land that is not yet his, about
which he knows little and that might provoke tremendous fear
in him.

There are several important messages about our own spiritual journeys in these stories. First, God's relationship with
Abram begins outside the Promised Land; each of us begins
our adult spiritual journey unsatisfied, not where we ultimately
wish to be. Second, God instructs Abram to risk virtually
everything he knows and loves for the possibility of a greater,
richer, more nurturing spiritual life; none of us should expect
the search for spiritual fulfillment to be simple or mechanical.
We, too, will have to risk. Third, God requires the Jewish people—the Children of Israel, the Strugglers with God—to wander for forty years after they leave Egypt; our spiritual journeys
are often not only difficult, but also lengthy. When we seek the
spiritual, we dare not expect instant gratification.

Fourth, and finally for now, we should not necessarily expect to feel, at any given moment, that we have "arrived."
Even after Abram accepts the challenge to leave his homeland
and to migrate to the Promised Land, he and his descendants
do not simply remain there. Scarcely two or three generations

after Abraham's journey, the Jewish people migrate again, this time to Egypt in search of food after Canaan is plagued by famine. Once in Egypt, they become enslaved, only to travel again as wanderers in the desert on their way toward the Promised Land.

"Toward" the Promised Land is the most crucial idea here. Even at the conclusion of the Torah—this "family diary"—the Jews have not entered the Promised Land. Moses brings the Jews virtually to the doorstep, but he is not permitted to usher them in. Note the last words that God speaks to Moses, indeed the last words that God utters in the entire Torah. We read:

> Moses went up from the steppes of Moab to Mount Nebo, to the summit of Pisgah, opposite Jericho, and the Lord showed him the whole land: Gilead as far as Dan; all Naphtali; the Land of Ephraim and Manasseh; the whole land of Judah as far as the Western Sea; the Negeb and the Plain—the Valley of Jericho, the city of palm trees— as far as Zoar. And the Lord said to him, "This is the land of which I swore to Abraham, Isaac and Jacob, 'I will assign it to your offspring.' I have let you see it with your own eyes, but you shall not cross there." So Moses the servant of the Lord died there, in the land of Moab, at the command of the Lord.
>
> (DEUTERONOMY 34:1–5)

We are, our tradition suggests, a people constantly searching for the Promised Land, knowing that the most enriching part of our lives may be this process of searching, not necessarily the exhilaration of arriving.

For Jews, the magic and the power of religious life is in the "quest." For us, what is most exhilarating, nurturing, and spiritually compelling about Jewish life is the enterprise of asking life's hardest questions, of searching for life's most elusive answers, and of building relationships with each other, with a

Force Jews commonly call God and with our tradition as we go through that process. The Gaon of Vilna, one of the great legal and spiritual minds of the early modern European Jewish community, was once asked whether, if he could receive infallible religious instruction from an angel, he would accept it. The Gaon said that he would refuse, because his life would be more meaningful and compelling if he struggled to find those truths on his own.

The Jewish tradition recognizes that to be a human being is to perpetually ask questions, to wonder without ever fully satisfying our wondering. Frustrating though many of our deepest and most personal questions are, we cannot put them aside, no matter how hard we try. Judaism teaches, in fact, that we ought not even try. Jewish tradition suggests that to be human is to wonder and to ask, to dream and to cry. To be human means resigning ourselves to the inevitability of not completely understanding the world in which we live, but at the same time committing ourselves to persisting in trying. Judaism does not demand that we have the answers; instead, it validates our struggles and encourages us never to give them up.

Far too often, we associate religious traditions with a catechism-like list of abstract and impersonal postulates that we imagine we are supposed to believe. But such a view misses the point of the dynamic, emotionally charged, and intellectually challenging conception of religious life that Judaism offers. As we have seen, even the Torah's most fundamental stories make that point; they suggest that being a Jew has never been a matter of passively acceding to a variety of religious propositions. Rather, being a Jew is about struggling to understand our place in the world, working to become more fulfilled human beings, and recognizing throughout that the process may be more important than the final product.

How do we conduct that search? How do we embark on the quest? The remainder of this book is dedicated to answering these questions. Each chapter will explore a crucial dimension of the traditional Jewish world. For many Jews, some of these elements have long seemed staid, irrelevant, or even oppressive. But I will seek to show that these worlds—of study, theology, prayer, law, community—are designed not to provide easy or facile answers, nor to control our lives, nor to convince us that Jewish life is about the blind acceptance of certain principles of faith. Rather, in each case we will see that the Jewish tradition seeks to validate and give honor to that part of our humanity that is always wondering and that is never satisfied. Judaism is about building community, fashioning relationships, creating meaning, and making life more fully textured than it would otherwise be.

Jewish life celebrates our humanity. It reveres the parts of humanity that wonder, that dream and mourn, that desperately want to love but cannot always feel the love they so desperately crave. The humanity that Jewish life celebrates, honors, and validates is the humanity of a people who have not had an easy or placid relationship with God, but who have a loving, questioning, doubting, struggling, sometimes even tormented relationship with God, with Judaism, even with life itself.

Judaism understands, deep in its soul, that the most profound of all relationships are relationships of struggle and growth. Our relationships with our parents, with our lovers, with our children, and with our closest friends are not always easy ones. But they are the most nurturing of relationships in our lives because they are the relationships through which we grow. They are the relationships in which we have the capacity to be the most honest, and as a result, they are the relationships that ultimately transform us.

That is what Jewish life is about. Our relationship with our tradition, its beliefs, and its demands is not an easy one, nor was it ever intended to be so. If those other relationships in our lives prove so fruitful precisely because they allow us to be honest and permit us to struggle, then Jewish life has to offer us no less.

◇

JUDAISM AND BELIEF IN GOD—CAN THE SKEPTIC EMBARK ON THE JOURNEY?

◇

JEWS OFTEN BEGIN THEIR SPIRITUAL JOURNEYS SOME-
what timidly. Implicit in their ambivalence is the common
question: "What do I have to believe to embark on the
odyssey?" "Is Jewish religious or spiritual growth going to demand that I stop thinking? Will I become a robot? A funda-
mentalist? What if I am not at all sure about God? Is there still
room for me on this search?" These are excellent questions,
natural ones. Is it worth "believing" in something you're not
certain exists? Is it even possible?

This natural hesitancy is exacerbated by modern culture. The world in which we live suggests to many Jews that doubt has no place in genuine religious or spiritual life. The images of religion that cross their television screens seem to associate religious passion with theological certitude. Much of what is mesmerizing about America's television preachers is their absolute self-confidence and their apparently unshakable faith in the "truths" they espouse. The reactions of their congregations, overwhelmed by the passion of the rhetoric and the power of the message, are often inspiring, almost hypnotizing.

But that sort of religious zeal is also foreign to many people. Numerous Jews, though anxious to embark on a Jewish odyssey and search for meaning, find such confident faith wholly alien, disturbing, even frightening. That sort of spirituality seems to dismiss the legitimacy of questioning. Even when they are anxious to begin their spiritual journeys, many Jews are simply not willing to dismiss their intellects and their questions. They want—they need—more than gifted preachers. They insist that wherever Judaism's spiritual journey takes them, it must not demand sacrifice of their intellectual integrity.

But Judaism, more than any other major religious tradition, does not see skeptics as second-class citizens. It would be difficult to imagine a committed Christian for whom some faith statement about Jesus was not a central religious tenet, or a Muslim openly skeptical about Allah. In that regard, Judaism is somewhat different. Judaism does not require faith statements as a sign of legitimacy. Judaism does not ask Jews to give up their questions or to deny their doubt. In Jewish spiritual life, faith is not the starting point of the journey. Uncertainty is not the enemy of religious and spiritual growth. Doubt is what fuels the journey. Indeed, as we will see, the Torah goes to great lengths to reassure the searching Jew that skepticism is healthy, legitimate, and even celebrated in Jewish life. Fundamentalists may regard anything short of absolute faith as religiously insufficient; Jewish tradition does not share their reliance on certainty.

Of course, the perception that belief in God is fundamental to authentic Jewish religious experience is not only the result of popular culture. Much of what Jews see about Judaism itself confirms that sense. After all, synagogue services constantly speak of God. The prayer book (the subject of Chapter Six) seems to assume confident belief in God. Almost all Jewish weddings make mention of God, as do naming ceremonies for children, the Passover Seder, Hanukkah candle-lighting ceremonies, funerals, and mourning rituals. Synagogue sermons tend either to speak of God as obvious fact, or to avoid the issue of God altogether. The result is that there are very few Jewish settings where Jews have the opportunity to wonder aloud about God, to articulate their sense of what they do and do not believe, and to share their frustrations at not being certain. Nowhere in their Jewish experience has Judaism provided a place to find reassurance that, in their doubt, they are not alone.

There have also been some strains of Jewish tradition that denied the value and legitimacy of skepticism. Maimonides (1135–1204) was perhaps the most prominent example, though by no means the only one. Judaism's greatest medieval philosopher, Maimonides thought that Judaism ought to have something akin to today's Catholic "catechism," a series of faith statements that would succinctly define what Jews ought to believe. He therefore composed his *Thirteen Principles of Faith* enumerating his basic theological convictions, beliefs he thought every Jew ought to share.

It is not difficult to understand why religious traditions tend to catechism, why they often create rigorous definitions of what they believe. One reason has to do with public identification as part of a larger group. Without catechism, what defines a person as a member of that faith? If Judaism so validates skepticism and searching, if it is not illegitimate to be uncertain about God, then what defines a person as a member of the

Jewish "faith community"? Surely it has to be more than birth. Toward the conclusion of this chapter, we will see that Jewish tradition was not unaware of this question, but opted for something very different than catechism.

There are also emotional reasons that explain why religions tend to enumerate distinct lists of beliefs. Many people—Jews as well as non-Jews—understandably find such certainty comforting. The world can be a very frightening place, and for some people, absolute belief in God's existence and certainty that God has a plan for each and every human being makes it possible to find the strength to go on. When such theological structures and belief systems provide comfort, there may be nothing at all wrong with them.

But not everyone reacts to the world in the same way. There are many other people for whom absolute religious certainty is simply not possible. Many people cannot assert with confidence that God exists, or that God has a plan for them, their people, or the universe. They cannot honestly recite Maimonides' *Thirteen Principles of Faith* as reflections of their own belief. The world these people witness seems unfairly cruel, and they find it difficult to accept the notion that in a "world to come," good people will be rewarded and the wicked will be punished. How does Jewish tradition make room for them? Where do they begin their Jewish spiritual search?

This chapter will argue that as important a figure as Maimonides was, Jewish tradition simply does not demand the sort of theological conviction that Maimonides espoused and that some Jews continue to find comforting. While it is true that many Jewish philosophers and some very important dimensions of Jewish tradition have long advocated precisely the certainty that Maimonides sought, and that the Torah and much of rabbinic literature take God's existence for granted, those dimensions of Jewish thought are not the only way in which Jews have viewed the world. Although Maimonides attempted to impose a catechism-like philosophic approach on Judaism, he was ultimately not successful. His *Thirteen Principles* are still well known and to this day are found in many prayer books, but they never became a catechism in most Jewish communities. They are studied and discussed, but personal acceptance of Maimonides' principles never became a sine qua non for Jewish legitimacy. Somehow, important streams of Jewish tradition resisted his approach. Those particular dimensions of Jewish thought may be especially helpful to Jews in modernity who still struggle with the whole idea of God.

In the following sections, we'll examine that dimension of Jewish life that not only permits, but even celebrates, a life of searching and of recognizing our skepticism. We'll see Judaism's tenuous balance between legitimating skepticism on the one hand, but insisting that we not dismiss God entirely on the other. We'll see a wide variety of traditional explanations of evil, and finally, we'll begin to turn our attention to the unique way of life that Jewish tradition provides to make meaningful living and spirituality possible even in the face of doubt.

THE JEWISH MOVE FROM BELIEF TO FAITH

How can Jewish life make room for skeptics? Why does Judaism validate doubt? Judaism takes doubt seriously because it takes people seriously. It recognizes that if Jewish life is to touch us, then it has to meet us where we are. That "place," Jewish tradition understands, is often a place of bewilderment, of hurt, of skepticism. It is often not a person's intellect but something less rational, more emotional, that prompts a spiritual search, and Judaism understands that.

Though there are many factors that motivate Jews to embark on spiritual journeys, Jewish tradition recognizes that, often, the most important factors are not cerebral. Sometimes, it is the grandeur of the universe that either provides a spiritual experience or motivates spiritual searching. A glimpse of nature more breathtaking than we imagined it could be. A simple unexpected kindness that so profoundly touches us that we begin to ask, "Who are we? Why are we here?"

Sometimes, it is the birth of a child. A child emerges into the world and despite the presence of nurses, physicians, machines, family, and all the attendant elements of modern delivery, we know that we are in the presence of a miracle. We gaze at our child and we recognize that all the biology in the world cannot explain this new being. We cradle in our arms not just another person, but a being of infinite value and vast potential. We cradle a piece of ourselves, and know that if we are fortunate, this piece of ourselves will survive us. Suddenly, we have a small piece of immortality. And we wonder: Who will remember us? How will we be recalled? After we're gone, will we and this child ever "meet" again? How? When?

At other times, it is trauma that motivates spiritual odysseys. Illness, death, loneliness—all of these also cause us to ask life's ultimate questions and to begin the quest for meaning. At still other points in life, it is neither celebration nor mourning that motivates our wonder. It can be a simple pause in the hectic pace of life. That moment when we have achieved most of the things that we planned to accomplish. All the needed degrees, a career, perhaps a family. The details vary with every person, but at some point in our lives, we may suddenly stop and realize that we've attained most of what we set out to do. Then what? Where next? What does it all mean?

Many people today begin their conversations about religion with the proverbial question "Do you believe in God?" But Judaism understands that if that question is the first one, then people who cannot answer yes will not be able to begin the journey. That is why the question "Do you believe in God?" is not the central Jewish spiritual question. It is not an illegitimate question; Jews are certainly not forbidden to ask it. But

Judaism has chosen a different emphasis, a focus not on belief, but on faith. Jewish life is interested not in proving God's existence, but in feeling God's presence. Judaism is interested not in philosophic arguments for God, but in what modern Jewish philosopher Abraham Joshua Heschel (1907–1972) called moments of "awe and wonder," moments when God suddenly seems close.

The unique qualities of the Jewish quest for God are reflected in many facets of the Jewish tradition, among them the spiritual poetry that has become an important part of the Jewish prayer tradition. Consider the following poem, which begins the Friday evening Shabbat service. *Yedid Nefesh*, a title that means "Beloved Companion," sets the stage for one of Judaism's most moving prayer services. As the sun sets, as a week of work and travail draws to a close, and as Shabbat begins, the poet expresses his most heartfelt wish. He writes:

> Beloved companion, merciful father,
> draw Your servant close to Your will. . . .
> My soul is weary and ailing,
> yearning for Your love. . . .
> Please, God, heal me. . . .
> Reveal Yourself to me,
> and spread Your canopy over me.

These yearnings, recited by Jews in every corner of the world each Friday evening, are not the abstract musings of the philosopher. They are the longings of a lover. Rabbi Eleazar Azikri (1533–1600), the poet who wrote *Yedid Nefesh*, is interested not in certainty or in philosophic inquiry, but in feeling God's closeness. "Reveal Yourself to me," he writes, "and spread Your canopy over me."

What this poem reflects, particularly in its images of father and lover, is not a philosophic, rational quest for God, but what many Jews call a "relationship with God." The phrase "relationship with God" is instructive because "relationship" does not imply certainty. "Relationship" implies gradual growth and learning with fits and starts, with periods of tremendous progress as well as deeply frustrating and painful times. Relationships develop, often unpredictably; Judaism's conception of how Jews come to know God is very similar. It is not certainty that Jews seek; Jewish life is about searching for God's sheltering nearness, a sense of God's presence, a glimpse of God's love. It is not an even, easy, or predictable road, but it is open to believers and doubters alike.

In focusing more on "relationship with God" than on "belief in God," Judaism differs from other Western religious traditions. While some Christian communities urge their followers, "Believe, and you will be saved," Judaism's rough equivalent is "Search, and you will find meaning." Jewish life certainly does not consider God unimportant; God is central to Jewish spirituality. But most of Jewish tradition decided long ago to focus not on essence, but on God's presence; Judaism seeks not God's truth, but God's closeness.

This notion is not new; it is not the product of Judaism's encounter with modernity. Indeed, this is the thrust of the Torah's description of Judaism's formative characters and their relationships with God. When the Torah applauds Abraham's developing relationship with God, it uses the word *he'emin*. The Hebrew word *he'emin*, though commonly mistranslated as "believed," actually means something closer to "trusted." When the Torah says of Abraham *he'emin*, it means "he put his *trust* in the Lord" (Genesis 15:6). Trust, relationship, feeling—and not proof—are what Judaism and Jews seek as they search for God on their spiritual journeys.

Nor is Abraham the only character through whom the Bible teaches that there are many different ways to God. One of the most beautiful tales about searching for God's presence is a story about the prophet Elijah in the Book of Kings. Elijah, who lived in the ninth century B.C.E. (about five hundred years after Moses), was a brooding, powerful presence, defending monotheism against King Ahab and the prophets of Ba'al. When the Queen, a Ba'al supporter, warns Elijah that she tends to kill him in revenge, Elijah flees to the wilderness, and alone he wanders fearfully for forty days and nights. Still in danger, with nowhere to turn and no one to help him, Elijah is on the verge of despair. He cries out to God, "I am moved by zeal for the Lord, the God of Hosts, for the Israelites have forsaken Your covenant, torn down Your altars, and put Your prophets to the sword. I alone am left, and they are out to take my life" (I Kings 19:10).

God seems sympathetic to Elijah's need, and responds to the lonely, frightened, and desperate prophet:

> "Come out," He called, "and stand on the mountain before the Lord." And lo, the Lord passed by. There was a great and mighty wind, splitting mountains and shattering rocks by the power of the Lord; but the Lord was not in the wind. After the wind—an earthquake; but the Lord was not in the earthquake. After the earthquake—fire; but the Lord was not in the fire. And after the fire—*kol demamah dakkah*, the sound of delicate silence. When Elijah heard it, he wrapped his mantle about his face and went out and stood at the entrance of the cave.
>
> (I KINGS 19:11–13)

Craving some sense of God's majesty and presence, Elijah receives what he needs. But his need to feel God's splendor is satisfied not by the mighty wind, the earthquake, or the fire, but by the *kol demamah dakkah*, the "sound of delicate silence." It is the intimate, gentle, almost silent moment in which something happens to Elijah. Something tantalizes and touches him. Something thoroughly nonintellectual enables him not to see or to hear—but rather to feel—the awesomeness of the God he so deeply loved.

Abraham's and Elijah's models of building a relationship with God without waiting for philosophic or rational proof are important correctives to modern Jews. They urge Jews not to wait for conclusive evidence before opening themselves to the possibility of God. When people make religion overly intellectual, the Torah and the Book of Kings suggest, their minds rob them of the opportunity to feel, to transcend the physical world, to sense something less tangible but perhaps more precious. Abraham's and Elijah's models urge modern Jews to set aside the quest for proof, and to begin the search for relationship. They remind us that sometimes we must stop thinking so we can begin to feel. Much of Judaism's unique way of life is geared to making that possible.

IS JUDAISM ANTI-INTELLECTUAL?

But isn't the move from belief to faith, from proof to relationship, intellectually shoddy? Isn't it an escape from the real issues? How seriously, one might ask, can anyone take a tradition that is not interested in proof and bases so much on intuition or feeling? Surely, for something as powerful as religion, for something as crucial as God, it seems natural that Jews should demand greater intellectual rigor. What does such an approach to spiritual odysseys suggest about Judaism's intellectual sophistication?

Jewish life takes the mind very seriously. Much of Judaism is a celebration of the intellect. In part, Jewish tradition claims, it is our ability to think, to analyze, and to reason that makes us human. As we will see in the next chapter, rigorous and intellectually sophisticated study is a crucial part of the Jewish spiritual odyssey. Nothing about Jewish life suggests that people should give up their intellectual skills, or stop thinking. For centuries, Jewish communities have reserved their highest accolades and their ultimate respect not for their political lead-

ers or financiers, but for scholars. Jewish tradition even suggests that the only person who could merit even more respect
than one's parent is one's teacher. Jewish tradition does not
denigrate learning, teaching, or thinking; indeed, it celebrates
them. There is nothing anti-intellectual about Judaism or Jewish spiritual quests.

But at the same time, Judaism asks us to think clearly about
the limits of intellectual pursuit. Judaism is sensitive to both
what the mind can and cannot do. While there is much that
the mind can accomplish, it is not only our mind that makes
us human. And for all that the mind can do, it cannot prove
God's existence or say with certainty what God is or what God
does.

For thousands of years, many human beings have been seeking to prove God's existence. Others have been trying, equally
unsuccessfully, to demonstrate conclusively that God does not
exist. But neither group has succeeded. So far as we know, the existence of God cannot be proven. The famed German philosopher Immanuel Kant (1724–1804) even claimed that he had
"proven" that God's existence cannot be proven. But by the same
token, no one can prove that God does not exist. Both claims are
claims not of fact but of faith. Both the person convinced that
God does exist and the person convinced that there is no God
are making faith-claims. Each is articulating a premise for which
there is no proof, but on which they base important life commitments.

It is not always easy to initiate a spiritual or religious search
without proof for God. Taking that step requires some risk.
Jewish tradition understands that most people would like
proof. Searches for spirituality—for God's presence and closeness—without proof make us vulnerable, open to disappointment. But Judaism insists that as difficult as risking may be, it
is necessary; there is no alternative. As we will now see, the
Torah's stories about Moses make precisely that point.

JUDAISM AND THE HUMAN DRIVE TO KNOW

The Torah clearly acknowledges that ours is not the first generation to want to know that the God we are seeking is not some figment of our imagination. From its very beginnings, Jewish tradition has understood that it is not easy for us to accept that God lies beyond proof, that faith in God is elusive. As much as we might be relieved to learn that our skepticism is not illegitimate, we are also often disappointed. That is why the Torah does more than simply assert that God is ultimately unknowable. The Torah takes pains to explain why certain elements of the cosmos—God in particular—must necessarily remain beyond the grasp of the human mind. Judaism insists that there is an important reason for our not being able to prove anything about God.

In its description of Moses' early leadership of the Jewish people, the Torah explains why God must remain unknowable. In the entire Bible, no person has a relationship with God more intimate than did Moses. He—and he alone—climbed Mount Sinai and spoke with God "face-to-face." One would certainly expect that were there ever a Jew who needed no more reassurance about God, it would be Moses. But the Torah suggests that even Moses, God's most intimate partner in the entire Torah, shared the craving for fuller knowledge and understanding of God that many modern Jews experience. Perhaps even more importantly, it explains why that thirst for knowledge can never be fully satisfied.

When the Torah first introduces him, Moses is tending his father-in-law's sheep in the wilderness. Alone, without anyone to reassure him, he wanders the barren hills of the desert, when he suddenly discovers a bush that is burning but is not being consumed by the fire. Amazed by the miracle, he slowly approaches the bush. Frightened, he turns away, afraid to look at what he is sure must be God.

Suddenly, God calls out to Moses, orders him closer, and then commands him to go to Egypt and free the Israelites. But Moses does not want to go. Though he has seen the miracle of the burning bush and has heard God's voice, doubt seems to plague him. He would like to be more certain. So he asks God, "What is Your name?"—imagining perhaps that hearing a name will enable him to understand better the God he is encountering.

God's response to Moses is beautiful, but enigmatic. The Torah says:

> And God said to Moses, "*Ehyeh-asher-ehyeh* [I will be what I will be]." [God] continued, "Thus shall you say to the Israelites, '*Ehyeh* [I will be] sent me to you. . . . This shall be My name forever, This My appellation for all eternity.' "
>
> (EXODUS 3:14–15)

What can God mean by that poetic reply? "I will be what I will be" can mean many different things. Perhaps it means that different people will perceive God in differing ways. Perhaps—though more problematic—it might mean that God is still becoming, and that any "definition" or name of God would therefore immediately be inadequate. There are many possibilities. Clearly, however, "I will be what I will be" suggests that God is ultimately unknowable.

Even Moses, the Torah suggests, could not know God. Even his spiritual search has to include moments of wonder, skepticism, and frustration. Doubt is an important—and legitimate—part of the struggle for faith.

This doubt and longing to know more continues throughout Moses' "career" and his developing relationship with God. Long after the encounter at the burning bush, when Moses and God have jointly experienced crisis, doubt, confrontation, threat, and reconciliation, Moses once again seeks a more permanent understanding of God. He pleads with God, "Oh, let me behold Your presence!"

Once again, God's response is highly instructive. After Moses' request to behold God's presence, the Torah continues:

> And [God] answered, "I will make all My goodness pass before you, and I will proclaim before you the name Lord, and the grace that I grant and the compassion that I show. But," He said, "you cannot see My face, for man may not see Me and live." And the Lord said, "See, there is a place near Me. Station yourself on the rock and, as My Presence passes by, I will put you in a cleft of the rock and shield you with My hand until I have passed by. Then I will take My hand away and you will see My back; but My face must not be seen."
>
> (EXODUS 33:19–23)

Can Moses really want to see God's *face*? The Torah has already told us that God spoke to Moses "face-to-face, as one man speaks to another" (Exodus 33:11). If what Moses wants is a physical glimpse of God, he should have been satisfied by this point.

Moses wants something more important—and more difficult—than merely seeing God's face. The Torah implies that he wants not to see God, but to understand God. He wants not physical sight, but a vision of the cosmos that enables him to transcend human beings' limited perspective. He wants to understand something that no human being before him had ever been permitted to fathom. Moses wants to understand not only God, but the workings of the universe. He wants the kind of understanding that will bring an end to his searching, his yearning, his doubt.

God's response to Moses virtually defines the Jewish quest for God. In this episode, God is more specific than at the burning bush. God explicitly tells Moses that he simply cannot have what he wants. When God says "man may not see Me and live," God is telling Moses that for him to have the understanding that he desires would be to transcend the human condition, to cease being a person. What God means is "If I grant you that request, I grant you divinity." One of Judaism's fundamental spiritual claims is that to be a human being is to wonder, to struggle, to yearn for understanding, but not actually to achieve it. For God's limitlessness far exceeds our capacity to understand. It was Yehuda Ha-Levi, the medieval Hebrew poet and philosopher, who perhaps captured the Torah's intention here best when he wrote, "If I understood Him, I would be Him."

At the same time, however, God does not completely refuse Moses' request. God does not say that wanting to know is illegitimate. God says to Moses, "You will see My back; but My face must not be seen." God suggests that there are many ways to know God. Even if Moses cannot see God's face, he can experience God's "back." Even if modern Jews cannot "know" God in a purely rational way, there are other ways to experience God and, ultimately, to know God. The Jewish spiritual search is about discovering those other approaches.

The Torah goes to great lengths to suggest that there is nothing wrong with the natural human craving for understanding, for knowledge, for the kind of faith that modern society commonly trumpets and televangelists claim to have achieved. The craving is natural, Judaism says. But it is also unrequitable.

Much of Judaism's spirituality lies in its celebration of life's mystery. Ironically, God might have been suggesting to Moses that if we were to solve life's great mysteries, we would also undermine spirituality. Judaism delights in life's mystery and revels in the unknown. As the sun sets Friday evening, the prayer book quotes the Book of Psalms 92:6 and exclaims: "How great are Your works, O Lord, how very subtle Your designs!" If we were to stop searching, we would also stop learning and striving. If Jewish life stopped pushing us to wonder, it would ultimately lose its relevance. The reason that so many modern Jews find nothing to draw them to Jewish life is that for many reasons modern Judaism has stopped touching those nerves.

Jewish spirituality is not about solving life's mysteries but about growing from them. That is why genuine odysseys are not always easy or even comfortable. But that is also why Judaism has so much to offer to Jews.

SUFFERING AND THE CHALLENGE OF FAITH

For some people, however, even the knowledge that Judaism does not require belief cannot address their misgivings about Jewish life. Simply seeing Judaism in part as a search for God's presence seems unacceptable. For the world they have seen seems incompatible with the notion of a just and caring God.

Nothing fuels our skepticism, nothing makes belief in God more difficult than human suffering. When children become ill or die, when we witness innocent men and women suffering, when disease takes those who should have had longer to live, God suddenly seems distant, cruel, or simply nonexistent. Where is God when innocent people suffer? What can Judaism do or say to make faith possible even in these excruciating moments?

Just as Jewish tradition offers no rock-solid proof for God, there is also no single explanation for evil that all Jews accept. Jewish belief knows of—and even legitimates—virtually all possible explanations. At one point, for example, the Torah suggests that suffering is the punishment for sin. In a passage that has now become part of the *Shema*, a central part of the Jewish liturgy, the Torah admonishes:

> If, then, you obey the commandments that I enjoin upon
> you this day, loving the Lord your God and serving Him

with all your heart and soul, I will grant the rain for your land in season, the early rain and the late. You shall gather in your new grain and wine and oil—I will also provide grass in the fields for your cattle—and thus you shall eat your fill. Take care not to be lured away to serve other gods and bow to them. For the Lord's anger will flare up against you, and He will shut up the skies so that there will be no rain and the ground will not yield its produce; and you will soon perish from the good land that the Lord is assigning to you.

(DEUTERONOMY 11:13–17)

This part of Jewish tradition suggests that God has a reason for everything, including people's suffering. Some people find this idea comforting, because it suggests a measure of control over our destiny. "If only I behave, I'll be okay," this theology seems to imply. For that reason, in Jewish circles no less than in Christian and other communities, the idea of reward and punishment still has its devotees. But many Jews are uncomfortable with this theology, for a variety of important reasons.

For some people, "reward and punishment" is a problematic explanation of evil because that theology denies the "evil" of suffering. While the belief in reward and punishment does not deny that people suffer, it insists that the suffering fits into a larger plan. The doctrine of reward and punishment denies that such suffering should not happen in God's world; rather, it insists that it must, because that is how God warns us and urges us to become better people. While the *theory* that people's fate is determined by their behavior is appealing, the examples of suffering that we often see—entire populations going hungry, or innocent children dying of diseases they certainly do not "deserve"—often suggest that some other explanation is necessary.

Jewish tradition has long acknowledged that reward and punishment does not adequately describe the world we witness. Even the Talmud speaks of "the righteous who suffer and the wicked who thrive" (Berakhot 7a). Therefore, the rabbinic tradition (approximately 200 B.C.E.–600 C.E.) explored other possibilities and explanations. Consider the following *midrash* (rabbinic narrative) based on the verse that reads, "Let us make man in our image":

> Rabbi Simon said: "When the Holy One, blessed be He, came to create the first man, the ministering angels divided into groups and parties, some saying: Let him not be created, and others saying: Let him be created. . . . Mercy said: Let him be created, for he will be merciful, and Truth said: Let him not be created for he will be all lies. Righteousness said: Let him be created for he will do righteous deeds; Peace said: Let him not be created, for he is full of strife. . . ."
>
> Rav Huna said: "While the ministering angels were still arguing and disputing, the Holy One, blessed be He, created man. Then He said to them: Why do you argue? Man is already made."
>
> (GENESIS RABBAH 8:5)

This tantalizing passage lends itself to a variety of interpretations, and raises almost more questions than it seems to answer. While on a surface level it seeks to explain the use of the plural in the phrase "Let *us* make man in *our* image" (which it does by adding the angels to the conversation, thus requiring the plural), other questions emerge. Why does Rabbi Simon specifically choose Mercy and Righteousness to support the creation of human beings, and Truth and Peace to oppose it? Is Truth's characterization of humanity "true"? Why did God not respond that humanity would, indeed, be truthful and peaceful? Could God create a truthful and peaceful human species? If that was possible, why did God not do it? If God could not do that, why not? And the questions go on.

But Rav Huna, in his addition to Rabbi Simon's tale, adds another twist. Why did God not wait for the angels' debate to get resolved? Would it never end? Or, perhaps, was God not fully in control? Some readers of this *midrash* believe that Rabbi Simon's intended message was that God could not create a truthful person, that God did not have the capacity to create human beings who would be wholly peaceful, and that ultimately, God could not have overruled the angels had they decided not to opt for creating humans. Therefore, this interpretation suggests, God went ahead and did it while they were not looking.

What does this have to do with the question of evil, the philosophic debate on theodicy? Perhaps Rav Huna meant to suggest evil exists because God is incapable of preventing it. A strange proposal, seemingly radical for a monotheistic tradition to make, but there we find it in the *midrash*. Not hidden, not discounted, but there for Jews to study, to read, to contemplate. What Jewish tradition has to offer is not a tendency toward blind acceptance, but encouragement of our struggles.

Another rabbi, named Shimon ben Yochai, went even further. His reading on the problem of theodicy was based on a different verse from Genesis, at the end of the story in which Cain kills Abel. After killing his brother, Cain runs away to "hide" from God. God calls out to him, and asks where Abel is. In a famous response, Cain asks, "Am I my brother's keeper?" God, responding to Cain's shirking of responsibility, answers: "The voice of your brother's blood is crying out to me from the land" (Genesis 4:10).

In response to this verse, Genesis Rabbah offers the following *midrash*:

> Rabbi Shimon ben Yochai said: "This is a difficult thing
> to say, and it is impossible to say it clearly. Once two ath-
> letes were wrestling before the king. If the king wants,
> they can be separated; but he did not want them sepa-

rated. One overcame the other and killed him. The loser
cried out as he died: 'Who will get justice for me from the
king?' Thus: 'The voice of your brother's blood is crying
out to me from the land.' "

(GENESIS RABBAH 22:9)

Rabbi Shimon ben Yochai's response to evil is even more sur-
prising than Rav Huna's. Indeed, that is why he begins his
midrash by saying, "This is a difficult thing to say, and it is impossible to say it clearly." For his proposal is both radical and
painful. In the analogy he creates between the two wrestlers
and the king on the one hand, and Cain, Abel, and God on
the other, Rabbi Shimon ben Yochai ultimately blames God,
not Cain, for Abel's death. Just as the losing wrestler cries out
and asks for vengeance against the king, Rabbi Shimon ben
Yochai says it is God who should take the blame. Just as the
king is cruel and merciless, he seems to suggest, perhaps evil
exists because God is in control, but God, too, is cruel and
merciless.

Though these explanations resolve some of the most obvious difficulties with the Torah's principle of reward and punishment, they are fraught with their own problems. Rav
Huna's notion that God is not entirely in control of the world
preserves God's goodness, but limits God's majesty. If God is
not in control, Who or What is? If God is not in control, why
pray? Can God answer our prayers? And how would we explain
the many other portions of Jewish tradition that insist that
God is absolutely in control?

Even Rabbi Shimon ben Yochai himself knew that his suggestion that God is cruel was an extraordinarily dangerous
thing to say. Recall his opening phrase: "This is a difficult thing
to say, and it is impossible to say it clearly." For obvious reasons,
the notion of a cruel God never became standard Jewish theology. A world ruled by a brutal God is almost too frightening to
conjure. Who wants to believe that we—with all our dreams,

accomplishments, fears, and disappointments—are little more than mice in the cage of a sadistic torturer? Who could go on to life's next challenges if it were all a cruel game? No one. For that reason, very few Jewish sources make the claim Rabbi Shimon ben Yochai is making.

Nonetheless, we should not dismiss Rabbi Shimon ben Yochai so quickly. For what may be his most important contribution to the Jewish discussion of evil is his conviction that even making a radical—seemingly heretical—claim such as his does not make a person's Jewish belief inauthentic. Rabbi Shimon ben Yochai was a rabbinic figure of major importance, and even his radical explanation of evil did nothing to lessen his status in traditional Judaism. All questions, and even radical answers, are legitimate in Jewish tradition.

Furthermore, Rabbi Shimon ben Yochai's *midrash* seems to suggest that it is better to be angry with God than to deny God. Surprisingly, he considered it preferable to voice his anger at a God he felt was cruel than to dismiss the possibility of that God altogether. Apparently, Rabbi Shimon ben Yochai, like all Jews, still wanted to be able to struggle for meaning, to find sense and majesty in the world. He was better off, he felt, expressing his hostile disappointment in God than in denying God a place in his struggles. Jewish tradition suggests that we would be wise to follow his model.

No discussion of evil in the Jewish tradition, however, could be complete without reference to one additional source. Jewish tradition actually devotes an entire book of the Bible to the exploration of suffering. That book, one of the Bible's most poignant, is the Book of Job. Job is not a Jew. His suffering is the suffering of all people, and it is profound. At the beginning of the book, he is healthy, blessed with seven sons and three daughters, and vast wealth. But as the story unfolds, he loses his wealth, his children perish, and he himself is afflicted with a horrible skin disease that causes him excruciating pain.

Job's wife, who is convinced of his righteousness, tells him that if God can allow him to suffer this way, life has no meaning, and that he should curse God and thus be killed, bringing an end to his torture. But Job refuses. His three friends, Eliphaz, Bildad, and Zophar, come to commiserate with him, but they suggest that he must have sinned somehow to provoke such an extraordinary punishment from God. But again, Job rejects that view, insisting that he has done nothing that could justify his profound misery. God, he contends, owes him an explanation.

At long last, after Job's long dialogues with his "friends," God answers Job out of the whirlwind, and says:

> Where were you when I laid the earth's foundations?
> Speak if you have understanding. Do you know who fixed
> its dimensions? Or who measured it with a line? Onto
> what were its bases sunk?
>
> (JOB 38:4–6)

Ironically, Job is comforted by God's reminder that his humanity limits his ability to understand. After almost forty chapters of exploring his suffering, the Book of Job concludes that understanding evil is simply beyond the capacity of human beings. And Job, according to the Bible, is comforted and dies contented.

Again, for the philosophically inclined searcher, the claim that God is beyond our understanding will seem unsatisfactory. That is why Jewish philosophers have explored evil and suffering in hundreds of Jewish texts and books. But what may be most important to our discussion is that none of those explanations became the authoritative Jewish stance on this complicated subject. Contrary to what many Jews imagine, Judaism does not have one authoritative answer.

Judaism's strength lies precisely in the fact that our tradition does not look for a single answer. The variety of Jewish answers assures us that no matter how angry or despondent we might become, those emotions do not place us outside the bound-aries of legitimate searchers. Whether we agree with Rav Huna or Rabbi Shimon ben Yochai, whether we find Deuteronomy or Job more appealing, one thing is certain: Judaism does not ask us to give up our questions, or even our anger. Doubt, frus-tration, and even fury can be legitimate parts of the Jewish spiritual search.

But at the same time, Jewish tradition insists that we must not give up the search. The tradition demands that we "stay in the ring," even if we occasionally get knocked down. In 1994, when the Union of American Hebrew Congregations (UAHC), the organizing body of Reform synagogues in the United States, refused membership to a synagogue that had deleted references to God from its liturgy, it did so in response to this part of the tradition. Surely, the UAHC was not sug-gesting that all Reform Jews needed to declare an absolute faith in God. But at the same time, however, the UAHC un-derstood that to give up the search would be to give up much of Judaism's richness and authenticity. In our darkest and most despairing moments, Jewish tradition urges us to light a can-dle, rather than curse the darkness. Judaism as a way of life is fashioned to make that possible.

NA'ASEH VE-NISHMA: THE JEWISH PATH TO FINDING GOD

But how does Judaism suggest we overcome the pain of pro-found suffering? How, in the midst of overwhelming loneliness and fear, do we search for God? Confronted with God's ulti-mate unknowability, how do Jews engage in a spiritual quest? Does Judaism offer anything unique as a means of working to get beyond our skepticism?

If Judaism is to be satisfying, it has to offer something more than wandering, something beyond wondering. Though Judaism's validating the search is important and refreshing, it is not enough. There must be some satisfaction from the odyssey. After all, no one wants to search forever. Jewish life has to offer more than struggle. There has to be more than a journey; we also need to arrive.

Nor is that all. Jewish life has to do even more than offer satisfaction on our spiritual searches. If Judaism is also to be relevant, it must also have something unique to say. If Jewish searches are indistinguishable from other searches, why Judaism?

This demand for something more tangible than "mere" searching is no modern creation; it is intrinsic to human nature. Even the story about Moses in the cleft of the rock suggests that the journey has to yield satisfaction. Though it is true that God cannot grant Moses' request to behold God's presence, God does say, "I will make all My goodness pass before you, and I will proclaim before you the name Lord, and the grace that I grant and the compassion that I show." Moses, at least, gets a response. He sees God's goodness, God's grace and compassion. God does not send him away completely empty-handed.

But we cannot duplicate that experience. We do not have the option of climbing back to the mountaintop to encounter God that way. How, then, do we work to meet God? What does Jewish life offer that is unique as we seek not only to search but to find as well? Does Judaism have anything to teach us about conducting the quest?

Not only does Judaism have something to say, it has a rather unique message. There is something particular about the Jewish spiritual odyssey. What is it? Again, the Torah suggests its answer in a story about Moses. This time, the incident takes place after Moses' encounter at the burning bush, but before his experience in the cleft of the rock.

After Moses' first descent from Mount Sinai, he assembles the people and recites at great length the laws that God had revealed to him atop the mountain. After hearing all these laws, the people respond, "All that the Lord has spoken, *na'aseh ve-nishma* [we will do and we will hear]" (Exodus 24:7).

Traditional Jewish commentators have explored the meaning of *na'aseh ve-nishma* in great detail. Sometimes, the tradition understands the verse as "we will do and we will hear," but at other times, Jews have taken it to mean "we will do and we will understand." Many questions have been raised about the passage. Why, the tradition asks, does "doing" come before "hearing" or "understanding"? One would expect the opposite. On a mechanical level, the people certainly have to hear the laws before they can perform them. But on a more philosophic level, why should performance of God's commands precede understanding them? Shouldn't understanding come first? Doesn't intellectual honesty mandate that we not accept the commands until we understand them?

In what has become a pivotal characteristic of Judaism, Jewish tradition insists that understanding need not come first. Tradition suggests that the Torah's peculiar language is instructive; it is no accident that the people first promise to act, and then say they will understand. The Torah's insight is that in the Jewish world of religion, study, and meaning, the feelings, the faith, and the spirituality we seek often follow behaviors specifically designed to elicit them. Jewish faith and Jewish spirituality do not come out of thin air, insists Jewish tradition. They come out of uniquely Jewish behaviors designed to let them grow and develop.

Rabbi Mordecai Kaplan fashioned very useful language for exploring this issue. He suggested that Jewish life revolves around three "Bs": believing, behaving, and belonging. He argues that for us, as we try to find a way into Jewish life, part of the challenge is to find the right place to begin. Should we wait to feel that we "belong" to or in the Jewish people, and *then* turn to either believing or behaving? Or should we first feel a deep sense of belief, and then create a pattern of behavior based on that belief?

Contrary to many prevailing views, Jewish tradition suggests that often what we believe or feel is a product of how we act. Strange though it may initially seem to us, Jewish tradition suggests that what we eat, the words we use, the clothing we wear, the amount of charity we give, and the ways in which we give it all have a direct bearing on what we will ultimately be able to believe. Our faith, Judaism insists, is in part a result of our behavior. That is how the tradition understands *na'aseh venishma*. And that is why, though it seems counterintuitive to many modern Jews, Jewish life suggests not that behavior should follow belief, but that belief—or perhaps faith, relationship, presence—is more likely to follow behavior.

Thus, Judaism insists that although absolute faith in God is not a necessary part of the journey, the journey has to include certain concrete steps to allow spiritual progress to take place. That is why the Jewish people at the foot of Mount Sinai said, "We will do and we will hear." What they really meant was "first we will act, and then we will understand." Jewish tradition claims that their message to modern Jews, inevitably still searching thousands of years later, is that spiritual progress requires spiritual work. Judaism's unique spiritual gift is its amalgam of concrete ways of life that are designed to foster not only wandering and the wondering, but discovery as well.

AESOP VERSUS THE MISHNAH

Twenty-five hundred years ago, Aesop suggested that "familiarity breeds contempt." Perhaps that is true in some areas of life, but it is not true with God. In a dramatic contrast with Aesop, the Mishnah insists that "the reward is commensurate with the effort" (Avot 5:22). Though the Mishnah was speaking specifically of study, the point is true of all spiritual enterprises. In spiritual life, familiarity breeds not contempt but comfort. The more people speak of God and wonder about

God, the less foreign God becomes, the more comfortable they feel.

If Jews want to recover spirituality, they will have to recover the meaning of *na'aseh ve-nishma*. We will get from Judaism what we invest in it. But American Jews are no longer used to investing in Judaism.

For all the richness and vibrancy of American Judaism, modern Jewish communities have focused on avenues into Jewish life that do not require tremendous investment and that do not make God part of everyday Jewish life. We concentrate on "social justice" but rarely invoke God in our discussions of what justice is. In order not to make anyone uncomfortable, many American synagogues minimize their discussions of God in services and sermons. Rarely do modern Jews who walk into a service hear that they are supposed to perform some distinctly Jewish ritual. American Jewish leaders have often assumed that overly demanding and overtly Jewish spiritual avenues would turn Jews away. They sometimes lose sight of the fact that Jews still yearn for spiritual growth and that many will work hard to achieve it.

The Torah's notion of "We will do and we will hear" suggests that we cannot simply will God or spirituality back into our lives. There is both comfort and challenge in Judaism's message about skepticism. The comfort stems from Jewish tradition's reassurance that "believing in God" is not an entrance ticket into Jewish life. There is no one specific faith-claim we have to make in order to start. And it is never too late. All we need is the desire to let Judaism take us on the journey. There is no creed we must accept. All we need is the desire to embark on the journey. Age does not matter. We might be college students, facing the world on our own for the first time, recognizing that life can be lonely and sometimes frightening. Or we might be "empty-nesters" beginning a new chapter of life, suddenly afforded the time and space to think about questions of life's meaning we'd never confronted before. Whether we are in college or old enough to have grandchildren in college, Jewish life is open to seekers wherever they may be.

But at the same time, Judaism's message is also a challenge. Genuine journeys are not easy. If modern Jews want Judaism to help them touch the spiritual, to transcend the world that they can see and touch, then they must play an active role. If they want to be able to answer the question "Why be Jewish?" honestly and passionately, they will have to search honestly and passionately. Judaism can enrich spiritual life only if we are willing to help and to invest in it. Judaism can bring Jews—all of us, regardless of age or background—back to God and back to spirituality, if we are willing to do the work. "We will do and we will hear," the Torah insists. Judaism will touch us, enrich us, help us transcend, only if we live it. The Jewish spiritual odyssey is not about blind faith. It celebrates the mind, the soul, and even the skeptic. But it also asks the skeptic to invest, to live fully, to participate in the richness that Jewish life has to offer.

CHAPTER THREE

JEWISH "CONVERSATIONS" AND THE WRITTEN WORD—LEARNING TO ASK THE RIGHT QUESTIONS

IF JEWISH LIFE IS A SPIRITUAL ODYSSEY, WHAT ARE our signposts along the way? How do we chart our course as we quest for spiritual satisfaction and meaning? Where do we do our exploring? One of the most important elements of Jewish spiritual searching, the subject of this chapter, is the encounter Jews seek with the written word.

In the preceding chapter, many of the claims about Jews and their search for God made reference to classical Jewish texts. Indeed, throughout this book, illustrations from sacred Jewish sources play a crucial role. Why is that? Why do these ancient texts play such a formidable role, not only in this book but in Jewish life in general?

When asked to conjure up a visual image of a Jew, many people respond similarly; the word "Jew" instinctively evokes images of books or sacred texts. "The People of the Book." Hasidic Jews dancing with the Torah scroll. A Passover Seder and its central symbol, the *Haggadah*. Prayer books, Bibles, elderly men huddled over ancient tomes. Even the discussion in the previous two chapters focused on stories of the Torah, our most central book. Almost every Jewish image and ritual seems centered around words and sacred texts.

Yet what does any of that have to do with life's spiritual search? For most modern Jews, these ancient tomes bring to mind irrelevance, obsolescence, and commitment to tradition at the expense of life in the modern world. These books have not touched their lives or the issues that matter to them. These books seem to assume values that we no longer share. They appear to dwell on the petty instead of the significant, on the trivial detail at the cost of the spiritual.

American Judaism has, with some exceptions, created a national network of religious schools in which children rarely get more than a fleeting exposure to traditional Jewish books. Many deeply committed Jews participate in Jewish works and causes almost daily, yet almost never confront a Jewish text in any serious way. As a community, American Jews have essentially decided that these ancient works are no longer key to Jewish "relevance," spirituality, or commitment.

Why, then, have Jews exhibited a passionate attachment to these works for so many centuries? Should we abandon that attachment? Could we not empower our modern spiritual searches by abandoning this detritus of an age gone by, this ballast preventing us from taking flight? Or do these texts still have some spiritual resource to share with us?

JEWS AND TEXTS: A TORMENTED LOVE

For most modern Jews, the mere suggestion that these ancient books might have some spiritual relevance today seems far-fetched. True, these time-honored books evoke an ancient, loving, and gentle world. Often, we see these texts and we imagine a way of life much less complicated than our own. Nonetheless, the world Jewish volumes evoke is not our world; it is not a world in which we personally would want to live.

In all probability, we would not choose to participate in that seemingly timeless way of life—in that world of ancient books and words—because our associations with it are not exclusively positive. This is true not only because for many of us the texts bring to mind irrelevance, obsolescence, and seemingly rote traditionalism. Other modern Jews, especially women, may recall the not so subtle but important point made by the opening of the movie *Yentl*. An itinerant bookseller reaches the village, and Yentl, a young Jewish woman desperately interested in traditional Jewish learning, longs to buy a book but knows she is not permitted to. She must confront the firmly entrenched barriers against women's studying Talmud and other classic Jewish texts. If these texts have for so long been off-limits to women, why would Jews with modern, enlightened outlooks seek to use them as a foundation for their investigation of Jewish life?

Still, the texts have a power all their own. Jews have clung to them with an intensity that seems almost strange. Consider the harrowing description of life in a Nazi death camp given by Professor David Weiss Halivni, perhaps this century's greatest Talmudist:

From Auschwitz, the 15-year-old Weiss was shipped to Wolfsberg, a camp in the Gross Rosen complex. Once, he saw an S.S. auxiliary about to eat a sandwich wrapped in what Weiss recognized as chapter 442, torn from the Lemberg edition of the Code of Jewish Law. Falling to his knees, Weiss begged to be given the wrapping, which he then read over and over and passed around to fellow Jews. The last one to have the chapter was a prisoner who collapsed and died during forced labor; the chapter went with him into the crematorium.[*]

A compelling image, this memory of a desperate need to hold the page, to touch it. We find ourselves amazed, perhaps even envious, that for some people, a fragment of paper and a few words could help to reconnect them in some small way with the world from which they had been stolen and which had been stolen from them.

But, many Jews have asked, when all else seems to have been lost, what is the value of a fragment of a Talmudic page or a remnant of an ancient legal code? Of what ultimate value is this retreat to words? What is the source of this Jewish infatuation with texts? Why is the reading of the Torah, the most ancient and sacred of Jewish texts, at the heart of the Sabbath service? Why do Jews turn houses into homes by affixing to every doorpost a *mezuzah*, nothing more than a simple container with a sacred text inside? Why do Jewish wedding ceremonies *require* a text—a *ketubbah*, or marriage document—to make the ceremony valid?

Why this centrality of the word in Jewish life? Texts, as we'll discover, are one of Judaism's most unique spiritual tools, its means of enriching modern life infinitely more than we might imagine.

[*]Israel Shenker, "A Life in the Talmud," *New York Times Magazine* (September 11, 1977).

JEWS AND TEXTS: AN ABIDING LOVE

Ironically, words cannot describe the Jewish love for words. The relationship between Jews and their classical texts might best be described as a love affair. The Jewish relationship with books is sometimes tempestuous, but it is also one without which Jews have decided they cannot live. The Jewish passion for books and words is no more easily explained than any other love; and love is not easily described.

And yet, we cannot desist; we continuously analyze our loves. Though we know words will fail us, we persist in trying. To adequately describe the spiritual odyssey that Judaism offers us, we must at least try to convey some sense, however inadequate, of what it is about books and words that Jews have loved for so long, and why they offer something so rich and compelling that many Jews simply cannot find elsewhere.

FIRST, A SENSE OF SAFETY

The origins of the Jewish infatuation with books and words are sometimes explained simply by Jewish history. Originally, Jewish religious life centered not on words but on geographic location. The primary focus of the Jewish religious expression was the Temple in Jerusalem. But would Judaism survive even if the Temple didn't? Scholars like Yehezkel Kaufmann suggest that when the Jews were first exiled from Judea in 586 B.C.E. and their Temple was destroyed, they recognized that if their religious life depended solely upon access to Jerusalem, they would not survive. Precisely at that point in Jewish history, Kaufmann suggests, the Torah text as we know it began to emerge as the central focus of Jewish religious life.

Scholars point to other historical examples in which the movability of the written word served as a key to Jewish survival. Roman rule of Judea had become oppressive and cruel long before the Judean community's leadership moved to Babylonia in approximately 220 C.E. But these leaders had hesitated to move from Judea to Babylonia (and thus evade the Romans, who did not rule Babylonia) because their oral traditions of law and lore had not yet been codified. The rabbis feared that leaving Judea would lead to the gradual loss of these oral and unorganized traditions. But once Rabbi Judah the Patriarch codified the Mishnah (a work in which he selected and organized many of these teachings) in 220 C.E., Talmudic authorities like Rav and Samuel suddenly believed in the possibility of Jewish continuity outside the land of Judea. So the locus of Jewish life moved east, avoiding the potentially insurmountable cruelty and repression of the Roman empire. It was the portability of the written word that allowed that Jewish community to survive. Indeed, Judaism not only survived; it thrived. The community that emerged in Babylonia after important scholars like Rav migrated there was more imaginative and religiously richer than the one that remained under Roman rule.

Jewish history is replete with other examples of the importance of the written—and portable—word in Jewish survival. When Jews were exiled from Catholic Spain during the Inquisition, they recognized that a phenomenally successful period of Jewish cultural and political life (often called the Golden Age of Spain) was ending. Many Jews had either been martyred or forced to convert to Catholicism. And yet, not all Jews despaired. We know from historical accounts that as they were exiled many carried their books with them. In their determination to ensure that their Jewish life would somehow persevere, they left behind their villages and their homes but kept their books, and thus their hopes to eventually revive Jewish life.

Jews, therefore, have come to love their books and the written word because these are the only things that could not be stolen from them. Even when books are burned or confiscated, words can remain—and do. Memory cannot restore life to the dead or rebuild destroyed cities and homes. But memory can, indeed, preserve the word. Despite exiles, confiscations, and deprivations, the written word has proved inalienable. No one can take it from us by force, so it has become even more beloved.

Not all Jewish communities can afford lavish synagogues. Some have even been prohibited from attending them. But because Jews have located much of their spiritual quest in the written word, Jewish spirituality has long been accessible to virtually every Jew who wanted it. Even in the repressive former Soviet Union, Jews who could not worship together or gather for communal celebrations managed to study. Small Jewish communities in the United States are also beneficiaries of this tradition. Even without the resources of larger communities, they can always get access to Jewish books, and, therefore, to much of the richness that Jewish life has to offer. Portability is no less important today than it was in the Roman empire. That is partly why texts are so central to Jewish tradition.

SECOND, A SENSE OF POWER

But there are other reasons for the Jewish preoccupation with texts. Jewish tradition knows the simple strength of words. In Jewish life, words are power.

Power may not be the first association we have with images of traditional Jews intently huddled around a volume of the Talmud. Indeed, the visage of the Jew lost in prayer often seems more passive than powerful, more submissive than imposing. The notion of words as power seems counterintuitive to moderns who readily revise the written word by computer, send it across the world by fax, and store it almost inexplicably as a series of ones and zeros on magnetic media. Words seem easily erasable, quickly replaceable. Modernity and its technology communicate the sense that words are cheap.

But the Jewish tradition insists that words do have power. It knows of the comfort we feel when people say the right thing, or how long we often recall an unsolicited compliment. Yet Judaism also recognizes how hurtful the wrong words can be, and for that reason regulates human speech in as much detail as it regulates any other part of our lives. Though words seem quiet, even ordinary at times, Judaism believes that in centering its spiritual search around words, it has selected a foundation more powerful than any other. Words, unlike other religious "artifacts," are also easily summonable. They are accessible to individuals and communities whenever and wherever those people want them. They cannot be stolen or destroyed.

The earliest Jewish sources express this sense of power in words. Consider the phrase repeated again and again in the opening of Genesis: "and God said, let there be . . ." God creates simply by speaking. Creation involves no tools, no implements, no visible acts of magic. The Jewish tradition suggests that the world itself was created with the power of words.

In fact, the Torah suggests that the entire content of God's revelation to Moses and the Jewish people on Mount Sinai was conveyed in words. The Jews assembled around the bottom of the mountain were terrified by visions of lightning and sounds of thunder. But God's communication to Moses at the very apex of the mountain was exclusively in words.

I noted above how affixing words to a doorpost in the form of a *mezuzah* transforms a house into a home, a shelter into a place to live and to grow. Indeed, words accompany virtually every major Jewish life transformation. A circumcision becomes a *bris* only when the surgical procedure is accompanied by certain words recited by the father and the *mohel*—the person performing the circumcision. Even if a ritually trained *mohel* does everything correctly, if certain words are not said, the obligation to have a *bris* has not been fulfilled. Similarly, men and women are married in Jewish tradition when the groom *says* to the bride, "Behold you are married to me with this ring according to the laws of Moses and Israel." Without those words, Jewish tradition does not recognize the marriage as valid. And tradition insists that a husband and wife are forbidden to live together for even an hour without a valid *ketubbah* (marriage document)—again, a contract made of words.

Jewish prayer, too, is exclusively a matter of words. In order to pray, the Jew has no obligation to be in a synagogue, no need for the presence of a rabbi. Sacrifice is long gone. Even prayer books are not necessary, and it is common to see traditional Jews reciting many portions of the liturgy by heart. Ultimately, Jewish prayer consists of words addressed to the Sublime. Even the *tefillin* (phylacteries—the leather straps and boxes) that traditional Jews wear during the morning weekday service are essentially enclosures for parchments upon which are inscribed biblical texts—words.

"A picture," the modern adage goes, "is worth a thousand words." Indeed, pictures *are* powerful. Many of us can recall glorious or horrifying news photographs long after we first saw them. But at the same time, photographs are limited in ways that words are not. It is much easier to tell someone a story that we have heard than to convey the power of a photograph. In order for a photograph to have impact on us, we need actually to see it. In order for a story to touch us, we need only to hear it. Words, much more than pictures, invite us to share. Words, much more than pictures, create communities because they can be summoned and conveyed so readily. And because they can be transmitted—and because we are often desperate to share them—words more than pictures build relationships. They build communities. They establish connection. They provide, in short, much of what Judaism needs to create lives of meaning and of spiritual warmth and richness.

THIRD, THE POSSIBILITY OF DISCOVERY

There is yet another reason for this love affair with words. In our encounter with words, we discover. We read the stories that our tradition tells about our origins, and we discover where we have come from. In the process of heated debate over the meaning of legal traditions, folktales, and poetry, we unearth pieces of ourselves and learn about those with whom we are engaged in debate. And as Jews have used words to describe their visions of the future—whether imminent or distant—we reveal our most passionately held convictions of the kind of place our world should become. That, says Judaism, is much of what spirituality is about.

Often, modern Jews express concern that Judaism's classical sources are no longer relevant to the lives of Jews on the eve of the twenty-first century. These books speak of stories we are not certain actually took place, or of laws that seem to have no place in the modern world. Of what value are such "fairy tales?" we often wonder. In its implied response to these questions, Judaism insists that there is more to "relevance" than we sometimes expect. If our traditional texts enable us to confront critical questions about the meaning of human life, Judaism claims, then these texts are not only "relevant" but have the capacity to be spiritually enriching as well.

To see how seemingly simple texts raise a variety of powerful spiritual issues, let's consider the story of the *Akedah*, or the "Binding of Isaac," from Genesis 22:

> Some time afterward, God put Abraham to the test. He said to him, "Abraham," and he answered, "Here I am." And He said, "Take your son, your favored one, whom you love, Isaac, and go to the land of Moriah, and offer him there as a burnt offering on one of the heights that I will point out to you." So early next morning, Abraham saddled his ass and took with him two of his servants and his son Isaac. He split the wood for the burnt offering, and he set out for the place of which God had told him. On the third day Abraham looked up and saw the place from afar. Then Abraham said to his servants, "You stay here with the ass. The boy and I will go up there; we will worship and we will return to you."

Abraham took the wood for the burnt offering, and put it on his son Isaac. He himself took the firestone and the knife; and the two walked off together. Then Isaac said to his father Abraham, "Father!" And he answered, "Yes, my son." And he said, "Here are the firestone and the wood; but where is the sheep for the burnt offering?" And Abraham said, "God will see to the sheep for His burnt offering, my son." And the two of them walked on together.

They arrived at the place of which God had told him. Abraham built an altar there; he laid out the wood; he bound his son Isaac; he laid him on the altar, on top of the wood. And Abraham picked up the knife to slay his son. Then an angel of the Lord called to him from heaven: "Abraham, Abraham!" And he answered, "Here I am." And he said, "Do not raise your hand against the boy, or do anything to him. For now I know that you fear God, since you have not withheld your son, your favored one, from Me." When Abraham looked up, his eye fell upon a ram, caught in the thicket by its horns. So Abraham went and took the ram and offered it up as a burnt offering in place of his son. And Abraham named that site Adonai-Yireh, whence the present saying, "On the mount of the Lord there is vision." . . . Abraham then returned to his servants, and they departed together for Beer-sheba; and Abraham stayed in Beer-sheba.

This simple but agonizing passage is almost omnipresent in Jewish life. First, it is recited once a year as part of the annual cycle of Torah readings. Second, the story was also selected as the Torah reading for the second day of Rosh Ha-Shanah, the Jewish New Year. Finally, and perhaps most significantly, it is *this* passage that the sages of the Jewish tradition selected to read at the opening of each morning's prayer service.

Why? Is the Jewish tradition suggesting that sacrificing our children is an ideal to which we ought to aspire? There are those who suggest that while Jewish tradition does not advocate (and indeed prohibits) the ritual sacrifice of children, Abraham's willingness to give up that which he loved most as service to God represents the ideal form of faith for which Jews can strive as they begin prayer each morning. Most of us will, thankfully, never know the agony a parent experiences when forced—or even asked—to sacrifice a child. Some traditional commentators suggest that this faith, a passionate belief that could lead a parent even to give up a beloved child, is the ideal faith we should have in mind as we focus our energies on the service about to begin.

Another explanation is that modern Jewish prayer replaced ancient Jewish sacrifice. Therefore, we begin our prayer service with a vivid, harrowing image of sacrifice in the ancient world to remind ourselves what our prayers have come to supersede.

But these two explanations do not do justice to the rabbis' intention: to fuel the process of discovery. The rabbis understood that the more we read this story, the more we discover that it is not at all simple. Myriad questions suddenly present themselves. When Abraham hears that God plans to destroy Sodom and Gomorrah, he defiantly asks, "Shall not the Judge of the world act justly?" Yet upon hearing that God wants the destruction of his own son, he is silent. He simply hurries to perform the command. Why?

After the angel of God commands Abraham not to sacrifice his son, the Torah tells us that Abraham returns to Beer-sheba. How do we explain that? Where was Isaac? Why does the Torah repeat "and the two of them walked on together" several times, but after the climax of this incident, no longer states that they walked together and does not even tell us that Isaac returned with his father? Does the Torah want to suggest that it is not necessarily true that "all's well that ends well"? Is the Torah trying to suggest that human beings have the capacity to sever relationships that nothing, even intervention from God, can repair? Is it possible that *this* is one of the messages our tradition sends when it places the Binding of Isaac at the beginning of the daily morning service? Those are the kinds of questions our tradition wants us to ask as we encounter these words. That is the kind of discovery this text makes possible.

Nor do these questions even begin to exhaust the subtleties of the *Akedah*. Why does *God* command Abraham to sacrifice his son, but an *angel* of God orders him to stop and bestows the passage's final blessing? Is it possible that Abraham has not passed the test but *failed* it? Might the tradition be claiming that before we run off ready to kill in the name of God's command, we need to wonder about what is right? How can we be certain it is God who speaks to us? How would we distinguish God's message from our own? Through words, and a simple story, comes the possibility of infinite discovery.

But we cannot stop here. The passage raises still more questions. Abraham and Isaac apparently never speak again after this incident. What do we learn from that? And God never speaks to Abraham again. What meaning can we derive from that? Why does Sarah, Abraham's wife and Isaac's mother, die immediately at the end of this story? What did she know? What did she sense? Was her world shattered? Why?

This process of examination leads us to uncover Jewish tradition's most important questions about human life. Judaism's sages might have suggested, had they glimpsed our educational world today, that too much of our focus is on "how to do" and too little is about learning "who to be." They would probably have felt that we concentrate inordinately on developing skills, training for a profession, attaining competence. But what about the broader issues of what kind of people we want to become, what values will shape our work in whatever profession we choose? How will we determine the commitments we would like our children to make? Those questions are matters of "who to be," and those are the queries that Jewish texts can help us begin to answer.

How should we learn who to be? Should we find teachers? Many of us have mentors; many more of us wish we had them. But even those of us with the good fortune to have the mentor know that her or his presence will not remain a constant. Teachers grow old, retire, and die before we are ready to say goodbye. Or we move away. And though we recall what those teachers have taught us, often with tremendous gratitude and even reverence, our dialogue with them almost inevitably ends.

But not so with Torah. And not so with the other sacred writings of the Jewish tradition. These sacred texts are one sort of mentor or teacher with whom our conversation need never come to a close. These "teachers," no less than the mentors of flesh and blood who play such pivotal roles in our lives, help us to discover life's most important questions, to guide our inquiry as we seek to discover who we want to become.

Perhaps even more marvelously, they are the very same "teachers" from which our grandparents, great-grandparents, and even great-great-great-grandparents learned. We are not the first generation to be frustrated at not understanding the universe; our great-great-grandparents no doubt experienced similar feelings. But how is our conversation a continuation of theirs? Do not the radical differences between our worlds separate us, almost entirely? No, they do not. When we speak of our frustration by invoking the image of Moses being told that he could see only God's "back," we continue a "conversation" that our great-great-grandparents may well have participated in.

Jewish texts are not only teachers. They are also "mentors" that connect us to a chain of people and to a tradition. They are not *less* powerful for not being physiologically alive, but rather take on a degree of permanence, majesty, and even sanctity. We sense that in confronting these texts and wrestling with them, we not only discover pieces of ourselves but join a profound conversation that has been going on for thousands of years. That sense of continuity and permanence is crucial to what Judaism has to offer. It is a sense that many modern Jews deeply wish they had. Jewish texts are one of the keys to creating it.

TEXTS AS ADMISSION TICKETS TO JEWISH SPIRITUAL LIFE

Precisely because the Jewish conversation about life's most important questions has been centered around words for more than two thousand years, it is virtually impossible to devise a uniquely Jewish way of engaging in such conversation without making use of texts. These volumes have become the "admission ticket" to Jewish spiritual dialogue. Without them, the dialogue might well be profound or productive, but it would be difficult to say that it is also palpably Jewish. Without text, what is uniquely *Jewish* about the conversation?

Hayyim Nahman Bialik (1873–1934), perhaps the greatest Hebrew poet of the modern era, lived thousands of years after the story of Abraham and Isaac became a centerpiece of Jewish textual life. Bialik, though schooled in these texts and a master of many of them, believed that Jews' infatuation with text had produced an anemic, passive, and self-deprecating Jewish sense of self that prevented Jews from defending themselves. Bialik believed that Jews had become so immersed in a world of words and the images they provoked that the reality of their lives and its horror was no longer apparent to them.

So how did Bialik make this argument to his listeners? Did he create a political manifesto in the tradition of Karl Marx? Did he compose a philosophical treatise like John Stuart Mill's *On Liberty?* or did he resort to some sort of political activism reflecting the newfound commitments of many of the nationalist movements of his own era?

No. Bialik knew Jewish culture well enough to sense that the only way to join a several-thousand-year-old *Jewish* conversation about the ideal nature of Jewish life was to join the chorus of words and images. He resorted to poetry.

In his classic and painful poem *The Matmid [The Diligent Talmud Student]*, Bialik evokes the profound loneliness in which he believes the *yeshiva* world has trapped its students.

> *. . . a human form—*
> *A shadow trembling, swaying back and forth,*
> *A voice, an agony, that lifts and falls,*
> *And comes toward you upon the waves of silence.*
> *Mark well the swaying shadow and the voice;*
> *It is a* Matmid *in his prison-house,*
> *A prisoner, self-guarded, self-condemned,*
> *Self-sacrificed to the study of the Law.*[*]

Is the image of the "self-sacrificed" young man a subtle allusion to the Binding of Isaac? Is the selfless devotion to the study of Torah—in Bialik's mind, at least—a continuation of the same dangerous pattern? Is Bialik trying to suggest that in devoting hour upon hour, day upon day, and year upon year to the study of the law, Jewish young men continue to relinquish their youth to the demands of cruel and inscrutable authorities?

Much later in the poem, as Bialik describes the disciple's master, he makes a more obvious reference to Abraham. He describes the master listening to his pupils studying:

> *And with a heart that fills with love, he listens,*
> *And hears the voice of his own boyhood, sees*

---

[*]*Selected Poems of Ḥayyim Nahman Bialik*, tr. by Israel Efros (New York: Bloch Publishing Company, 1965), p. 29ff.

> *Once more the long chain of his earthly years;*
> *And while remembrance wakes, his old eyes fill*
> *And two tears fall upon his silver beard . . .*
> *Why does your heart weep, old graybeard? Is the boy*
> *The mirror of your years of countless sorrows?*
> *Do you see again the day you went forth*
> *From home and from the city of your birth?*
> *Do you remember your days of loneliness,*
> *Your boyhood, and your boyhood's hungry years?*

The master's tears, Bialik suggests, come from his own sense of loneliness, his recollection of his own uncelebrated youth. And to evoke the image of a tradition that almost violently pulls us away from our roots, Bialik refers to Abraham, to whom God had said, "Go forth from your native land and from your father's house to the land that I will show you" (Genesis 12:1).

Earlier, I suggested that the image of Abraham being told to wander is the Torah's powerful way of suggesting that Jewish life is about a quest. Here, Bialik uses the same image for wholly other purposes. Now, Abraham's wandering symbolizes not quest and searching but the suffering of a young person viciously torn from his home and the youth he should have had.

Bialik joins the historic Jewish conversation from within. To suggest that our love of these texts has become profoundly problematic, Bialik finds himself turning to metaphors that emerge from those very texts he finds oppressive! The images are so deeply ingrained in both Bialik and his readers that they become the most powerful way to convey his ideas.

We, too, know of words that provoke powerful and emotional responses. For Americans, the phrase "I have a dream" evokes images of race, struggle, mass demonstrations, suffering, and loss. When we hear those words, we have no need for an explanation of who said them, or what his struggle represented. The mere words summon associations with the turmoil of that era; as we recognize that we require no explanations, we also come to appreciate the depth of our American unconscious.

The same is true for Bialik, his readers, and countless Jews throughout the ages. The words "Go forth from your native land and from your father's house" were powerful precisely because everyone recognized them; as they heard them, they encountered the depths to which Jewish idioms had burrowed deep into their souls. The image of Abraham makes the conversation—and even the stinging critique—a Jewish one. It defines both the speaker and the listeners, even if they disagree, as part of the same ongoing dialogue.

Jews—even modern Jews—study these texts because they are our way into this conversation. In opening up these books and exploring their meaning with other human beings, we join the timeless dialogue about who and what we want to be. Those are the questions that serious Jewish education would have us ask. Our tradition suggests that becoming "Jewishly educated" is not merely becoming familiar with holidays, traditional texts, Jewish philosophy, or culture; it is a matter of bringing these traditions, texts, metaphors, and insights to bear on our modern and timeless struggle to discover who we want to become.

In this respect, the Jewish notion of the "educated person" is not unique. Western colleges and universities require students to read the great works of authors such as Plato, Aristotle, Aquinas, Augustine, Machiavelli, Nietzsche, Freud, and Arendt not because these authors represent interesting footnotes to the history of European civilization, but because the faculties of colleges and universities have long seen these authors and philosophers as crucial components of an enduring conversation about the fundamental values of Western civilization. Many North American colleges have returned to the conception of a "core curriculum" precisely because they believe that there are central questions that need to be asked before a person can be called educated.

So, too, with Jewish tradition. In encountering Jewish texts, Jews seek to examine and articulate the fundamental tensions and conflicts in human life. That is why the discovery of our collective diaries is so important and so urgent. When the Torah tells the story of our ancestors, we discover that the questions that perplex us, the ones that shape our spiritual odysseys, are not new. We discover in grappling with Jewish texts that our fundamental questions are perennial; we learn that the human condition is not a modern condition but a timeless, existential one. And we learn that being Jewish is most profoundly about thinking through the questions that the human condition begs us to ask.

This notion of the power of an enduring conversation is radically new to many of us. But we need to confront it, for if we close ourselves off from these texts, we block ourselves from embarking on the distinctly Jewish spiritual odyssey we yearn for.

PICTURES OF THE TEXT

Consider two pages: one, a page of a typical modern book; the second, a page of Talmud. Perhaps because this sense of how Jews read and "hear" texts is so profoundly different from the ways in which modern women and men think about the written word, it would be helpful to illustrate the way in which the unique appearance of traditional Jewish texts contributes to this "sacred dialogue." Unlike the words on this page, which are neatly aligned and are exclusively the product of one person's work and thought, the page of a traditional Jewish text typically represents the thoughts, ideas, and dreams of Jews over many centuries. In some respects, we might compare the work of a modern Western volume to the melodic theme played by a soloist; the traditional Jewish text, in this analogy, might be either the harmony and power of a full symphony or, at other times, the cacophony of competing and passionately dissenting voices.

Notice how different the Talmudic page is from a page of a modern English book. On one page of Talmud we find: biblical quotations thousands of years old, a selection of Mishnah codified by Rabbi Judah the Patriarch of the Palestinian Jewish community in approximately 220 C.E., sections of the Babylonian Talmud that reached their latest stages of formation in Babylonia three or four hundred years after that, the medieval commentary of Rashi from the south of France in the eleventh century, the commentaries of other European scholars known as the Tosafists, and commentaries by several others who wrote in the early modern period.

Even the layout symbolizes dialogue. The Jewish conception of learning is not a unidirectional transmission of information from the teacher to the learner. Rather, the design of the Talmudic page suggests that we learn by struggling, debating, and even arguing. We learn by listening not only to the earliest of voices or to the most modern ones, but by exposing ourselves to the positions, opinions, and convictions of people from all over the world and in many different centuries. That is the case because Jewish learning is ultimately not about the accumulation of knowledge; it is about garnering spiritual insight. Ultimately, we learn not to be told how to *do*, but to discover who to *be*.

Jewish learning spaces are different, too. For the most part, university libraries are quiet places, where the more serious the library's clientele, the quieter the atmosphere. These libraries convey the sense that we learn best, we think most clearly, we absorb the most when no one interferes with us. Our educational and intellectual task could be most effectively accomplished, the Western world suggests, if only we could be left alone in perfect silence in the company of our books and our notes.

הזהב פרק רביעי בבא מציעא ס

וְאֵין ל"ג חדשים בישנים · משום דאמר בפ' המוכר את הספינה (ב"ב דף צח.) דכל מילי עתיקי מעלו לבר מתמרי שיכרא ומילחא:

[מַאן] (אבל) נותן לו לתגר. דאפייה אסר שלא להכניסן · רבא אימו לרבי זריקא. נרסינן לאחשבין שהם מזונין משום כדאמרינן בנדרים (דף נט.)...

...ואין צריך לומר חדשים בישנים **באמת** אמרו בין התירו לערב קשה מפני שהמשכירין אין מערבין שמרי יין בין אבל נותן לו את שמריו ימי שנתערב מים בינו לחבר אע"פ שהודיעו שאינו אלא ולא הודיעו לחבר שהוא אלא לרמות מה שדורות...

הדרן עלך הזהב

מַתְנִי' רבי יהודה אומר לא יחלק החנוני קליות ואגוזין לתינוקות מפני שהוא מרגילן לבא אצלו וחכמים **מתירין** ולא יפחות את השער וחכמים אומרים זכור לטוב מפני שהוא מגרים דבר אבא שאול וחכמים מתירין לומדים שלא יבור מעל פי מגורה שאינו אלא כגונב את העין אין מפרכסין לא את האדם ולא את הבהמה ולא את הכלים:

גְמ' מאי טעמייהו דרבנן **דאמר** ליה זכור לטוב וכו': מאי טעמא דרבנן משום...

הזהר   פרק רביעי   בבא מציעא

Two pages from the Babylonian Talmud—Bava Mezia 59b–60a.

Not so in the Jewish world. The typical modern *yeshiva* (academy), whether in North America or in Israel, whether in Eastern Europe several hundred years ago or in Jerusalem today, is distinguished not by silence and calm but by boisterous and energetic argument. While the Western library typically provides study carrels that shield one reader from the other, a *yeshiva* often has no furniture beyond long tables and the chairs surrounding them. The students of the *yeshiva* are not shielded from one another; in fact, their physical proximity to one another virtually forces them to listen, to respond, to hear, to rebut, and to emerge from the encounter enriched not only by the book but by fellow human beings who have their own reactions to it.

Traditionally, Jews do not study alone. In almost every traditional Jewish learning setting, students are immediately assigned—or find for themselves—a study partner known as a *havruta*. The *havruta* is more than a study partner. The *havruta* becomes the person with whom the student embarks on an odyssey that incorporates not only intellectual growth but also spiritual searching. Because the texts of the Jewish tradition touch so profoundly on the most intimate and personal of spiritual issues, no real *havruta* partnership remains limited to formal study hours. In traditional settings, where *havruta* partnerships typically last for years, the two partners often come to know each other as well as they know their closest friends or even members of their families. For them, there is nothing dry or purely theoretical about the study of Torah. Rather, study partnerships such as these evoke the traditional Jewish conception of Torah that declares that it is a "tree of life to them that cling to it" (Proverbs 3:18).

And so we return to the Jewish love affair with text. Like real human relationships of love, it is tumultuous, unpredictable, virtually addicting. Like real human passions, Jewish love for the written word pervades every crevice of the lover's life, leaving no aspect of her or his life untouched. And as is the case with love relationships that work, the lovers in this relationship also understand that without their cumulative experiences, they would not be the people that they have come to be.

THE TEXT AND THE CHALLENGE

Still, these texts frighten many of us. Precisely because they *are* so different in their construction, their language, their vocabulary and rhetoric, they often seem impossible for us to penetrate. Is the effort worth it? Is it possible for adults who have not previously been exposed to this type of study to make headway in these texts? If much of Judaism's intellectual openness and spiritual richness is located in this part of the tradition, can we participate in it?

The most common answer is no. We assume that Jewish texts are so difficult, and the challenges to understanding them so formidable, that we might just as well not begin.

Jewish tradition recognizes how discouraging these texts can seem. Long ago, Jewish communities developed a tradition that every volume of the Talmud starts on page two. Why is there no page one? Because, our tradition suggests, no Jew is a rank beginner.

Traditional pagination probably has other historical origins; still, this popular tradition is lovely. It is profound because it recognizes that even if we do not yet possess the linguistic or grammatical skills to parse these texts in the original, each of us brings something unique to the reading of these texts because we have lived, loved, dreamed, and endured disappointments. Reading them in our native languages is also a legitimate way to begin. Our tradition wants us to recognize that at the moment that each of us begins to struggle with these texts we each have something to say about them that no one else in the world can say. No one else can see these texts through precisely the same lens that we do. Thus, our contribution to the dialogue is not only legitimate, it is essential.

These texts are difficult, but they are our ticket into Jewish authenticity. Without them, we must always ask ourselves what makes our religious lives and our spiritual searches uniquely Jewish. Other religious traditions and many nonreligious schools of thought engage in serious spiritual pursuit. What makes the Jewish spiritual pursuit uniquely Jewish is that it is framed by these texts. Without these texts as our core, we become what Paul Cowan calls "orphans in history." We end up somewhat uncertain from where we have come and who, ultimately, we are.

There are a multitude of ways to frame a spiritual search. Judaism begins its search with *talmud torah*—the study of Torah— because it believes that formulating productive spiritual questions is done best by confronting the texts of a tradition that stretches back for thousands of years. Is this the only way to embark on a spiritual search? Certainly not. Is the student who claims that she finds the same meaningful questions raised in Shakespeare somehow mistaken? Of course not. Is this confrontation with Jewish texts even the *best* way to begin a spiritual odyssey? Not necessarily. So why is it the way that Jews cling to so energetically?

Because it is *our* history. It is not necessarily a better way, but it is *our* way. This is what makes a spiritual odyssey a *Jewish* spiritual odyssey.

Talmud torah, the Jewish tradition of encounter with the written word, is what makes our search a Jewish search; it is what links Jews across the globe in their ongoing searches. It is Judaism's way of celebrating the mind and the intellect; it is what guarantees Judaism's intellectual sophistication and integrity. I suggested in Chapter Two that Judaism does not demand that we give up our intellectual pursuits. Here, however, the claim is even stronger. Judaism wants Jews to celebrate their intellect, to make Judaism a profoundly intellectually satisfying experience. Texts are the guarantor of Judaism's richness, vitality, and ultimately, its spirituality.

If we want to experience the depth of Jewish spiritual life, we will have to make these texts our partners. We need to rediscover the stories our ancestors have been studying for centuries, not just because they are "Jewish," but because they help us ask important questions. As we wonder what we can truly know about the world, we need to ask what it means to see only God's "back." As we struggle with questions of what determines what is truly just and moral, we ought to ask ourselves what Abraham's experience upon being told to sacrifice his son might teach us. As we wonder whether we ourselves will ever be witness to miracles, we should let the story of Hanukkah speak to us about not only a cruse of oil that burned longer than expected, but the life of a people whose survival seems to have transcended all odds. Without words, we cannot ask these questions as well. But with words, and with distinctly Jewish texts, Judaism has the capacity to nurture our questions and our searches more than we might ever have imagined.

If texts are the first major building blocks of the Jewish spiritual journey, what comes next? If texts give expression to the rational, intellectual portion of our journey, where does Judaism make room for the more purely emotional? A very important part of the Jewish spiritual odyssey is the world of ritual. Let's turn to that world now, as we discover yet another way in which Jews embark on their searches and as they look to Jewish life to provide life's most spiritual moments.

RITUAL—

CREATING SPACE

FOR SPIRITUALITY

POWERFUL AND MOVING AS STUDY CAN BE, JUDAISM has to do more than challenge us intellectually. If it is to help us search for spirituality and quest for a sense of God's closeness, Jewish life has to give us opportunities to express hope and fear, joy and grief. It has to connect us not only to tradition and to our history, but to family and community. It has to create moments in which we touch the innermost parts of who we are, when we can appreciate the miracles of everyday living and when we can reconnect to the dreams we have for ourselves, our families, and the world. Judaism, if it is to provide Jews with something that will truly shape their lives, has to make room for the soul no less than for the mind. That is why, in addition to the world of words and text, Jewish life also revolves around ritual.

Many Jews find it difficult to imagine that Jewish ritual could be emotionally compelling or spiritually gratifying. Their own experiences with Jewish celebrations have been anything but rewarding. They remember Passover more as a family obligation than as an evening devoted to profound thinking about the meaning of freedom. Sometimes the Seder seems to represent oppression more than it does liberation. Hanukkah seemed more an imitation of Christmas than a spiritual moment that could touch adults. Candles were lit and presents distributed without anyone's having spoken of issues that truly matter in human life. Hanukkah, like the Seder, seemed more like something we are "supposed" to do than a festive occasion that has something significant to say or to teach. Other examples abound. For many modern Jews, Jewish ritual seems contrived, superficial, and, ultimately, irrelevant.

Nonetheless, many formerly secular or unaffiliated Jews are returning to the world of Jewish ritual, not primarily out of a sense of obligation but because they find that Jewish life moves them as nothing else could. Often, those Jews are coming back to the traditions of Jewish life after giving up on Jewish life, or even after having sought meaning and spiritual fulfillment in some other tradition. Why are they coming back? What is touching them? What have they discovered in Judaism's ritual life that they did not find elsewhere?

These questions do not lend themselves to simple answers. Somewhat surprisingly, classical Jewish texts are not particularly self-reflective about how ritual works. It is difficult to point to Talmudic discussions of why individual rituals are so emotionally compelling. While many Jewish legal treatises discuss how to perform the rituals, they rarely ask why.

Much of that silence is due to classical Jewish theology. Because traditional Jews have long believed that Jewish rituals were commanded by God, there was relatively little need to justify them or to wonder how and whether they "worked." Simply knowing that God expected Jews to perform them was enough.

Today, of course, many Jews understandably demand more conceptual explanations for Jewish ritual. Many Jews find the theological certitude of their ancestors elusive. They are not as convinced that God actually commanded them to perform these rituals. Therefore, Jews in recent years have explored in greater depth the meaning not only behind Judaism's individual ceremonies and customs, but behind the entire amalgam of practices known as Jewish ritual. Throughout this chapter, we'll examine some of the ways in which Jewish ritual works, and will see that traditional ritual is one important dimension of Judaism's attempt to foster lives that are thoughtfully examined and imbued with meaning.

As we examine the world of Jewish ritual, we should not anticipate one authoritative reason for each ceremony or custom. Just as each Jew who studies a classical Jewish text reaches different conclusions about its meaning and is touched in profoundly personal ways, so, too, each person drawn to Jewish ritual is drawn by something slightly different. The wisdom of Jewish ritual is that it works on many different levels. Often, it functions in different ways for even the same person. What draws a person to the rituals of Jewish living now may not be what attracted them just a few years ago. The dimension of Shabbat that touches them today may not move them in quite the same way a few years from now. Today, it might be the interpersonal dimension of Shabbat—the image of blessing children and of shared family time that touches them—while years from now, it may be the ritual of Shabbat—candles, the song, and the distinctly slower pace of the day—all providing an otherworldly sense of tranquillity and permanence, that seems most alluring.

Yet somehow the power remains. How does this happen? How does ritual enrich the lives of Jews? Is it the symbols of the ritual that evoke their power, or are its words also important? Are Judaism's ritual and intellectual traditions unrelated, or is there some connection between them? How does ritual contribute to Judaism's intellectual coherence? Those are some of the questions this chapter addresses.

RITUAL AS THE SOURCE OF CONNECTEDNESS

As we have been discovering, much of the spiritual power of Jewish life stems from the various sorts of connections that it fosters. *Talmud torah* (the study of sacred texts) creates a connection between Jews today and the countless Jews of the past who wrestled with the same words, who struggled with similar quests for meaning. Ritual, too, is largely about the creation of connections. In ritual, however, these are connections not only to Jews of the past. Jewish ritual creates connections to other Jews, to people and to central ideas in Jewish life. Though we rarely expect this of ritual, it establishes links to the issues of ultimate importance that give human life and Jewish living their real meaning. Let's begin our discussion of ritual by looking at some of the ways it creates connections to other people.

RITUAL AND CONNECTIONS TO PEOPLE

Perhaps the most widely known ritual in Jewish life is Shabbat. On a "technical" level, Shabbat is about creating a day of rest in commemoration of God's rest after the Six Days of Creation. As the Torah clearly explains, God commanded that:

> the Israelite people shall keep the Sabbath, observing the Sabbath throughout the ages as a covenant for all time:

it shall be a sign for all time between Me and the people
of Israel. For in six days the Lord made heaven and earth,
and on the seventh day He ceased from work and rested.

(EXODUS 31:16–17)

According to this view, Jews do not cook, use fire, build, destroy, shop, or go to work on Shabbat because these activities
are all derivative of the Torah's conception of work. Just as
God ceased working on the seventh day, Jews abstain from
work on Shabbat.

While this explanation of Shabbat is important, it also fails
to inspire many Jews. They wonder: How am I to take this idea
seriously if I'm not convinced that the world was created in six
days? Why should I take a huge portion of my precious free
time and adopt all these constraints? Why should I "imitate"
what God did? Aren't there more important elements of Godliness that I would be better off emulating?

These are important questions, but they miss part of the
point. The idea of Shabbat is not simply that imitating God is
important for its own sake. Rather, Shabbat insists that this
"imitation" has important spiritual and emotional implications for the people involved in it. How? One implication is
the element of connection. Indeed, Shabbat is largely about
connection. Shabbat gives Jews a chance to appreciate the
people who give meaning to their life.

As we will see later in this chapter, Shabbat functions on
other much more subtle levels as well. But for many Jews, no
matter how Jewishly learned or accustomed to Shabbat they
may be, what remains compelling about Shabbat are the connections and relationships that it renews and reinvigorates.
Newcomers to a traditional Shabbat evening meal are often
struck not by the theological or overtly religious elements of
the evening, but by the simply human dimension of Shabbat.
What stays with them is the simple sight of parents placing
their hands on children to bless them, or of a husband singing

a song of praise and love to his wife. The memories that linger are those of families gathered around a table singing, of genuine celebration and festivity somehow created in the very midst of a hectic and often numbing pace of life.

With time, what many Jews discover about Shabbat, a day that Abraham Joshua Heschel called a "palace in time," is the irony that its restrictions are ultimately liberating. While many people commonly complain that a day on which they cannot work seems overly restrictive, Jewish tradition has come to see Shabbat as a day on which we are freed from working. In an age of fax machines, car phones, pagers, and other gadgets that seem to find us wherever we are and that seem to suggest that everything is an emergency, Shabbat suggests that virtually nothing is that urgent. The genius of Shabbat is that it restores a sense of values and priorities. It "forces" Jews to leave their computers and offices, thus reuniting them with friends and family members who more urgently need their attention, their company, and their devotion.

Ironically, because they "cannot" work on Shabbat, Jews experience themselves as freed from having to work. Because their tradition "commands" this day and its particular spiritual qualities, we are somehow forced to undergo a change we know we need. No one puts it more poetically than Heschel:

> The seventh day is the exodus from tension, the liberation of man from his own muddiness, the installation of man as a sovereign in the world of time. In the tempestuous ocean of time and toil there are islands of stillness where he may enter a harbor and reclaim his dignity. The island is the seventh day, the Sabbath, a day of detachment from things, instruments and practical affairs as well as of attachment to the spirit.[*]

[*]Abraham Joshua Heschel, *The Sabbath* (New York: Farrar, Straus and Young, 1951), p. 29.

In its emphasis on familial and communal celebration, the modern observance of Shabbat transforms "imitation" and turns it into connection. It fosters Judaism's spiritual richness by creating a way of life that virtually ensures that we will embark on the journey in the company of other people, searching and yearning as we are.

Shabbat is not the only ritual in Jewish life that fosters relationship and connection. While each life-cycle ritual (the *bris*, naming ceremonies for girls, weddings, funerals, and the like) has its own symbolism and its own message, and each holiday on the annual calendar cycle (Rosh Ha-Shanah, Yom Kippur, Sukkot, Passover, Shavuot, and the others) celebrates a different value or event, what ultimately makes them powerful is the sense of community that they provide. Sharing many of these holidays and life-altering moments together somehow creates the connectedness that many modern Jews desperately want but have not found elsewhere. When they finally find that connection, they find spiritual richness, a sense of intimacy. They find meaning.

There is an intimacy to sharing in naming a friend's baby. There is warmth and a sense of connectedness to be found in spending Sukkot afternoon in a fragile booth, singing, studying, and interrupting life's other commitments simply to celebrate and rejoice. It is no accident that Judaism encourages a *minyan*, or prayer quorum, for circumcisions and weddings. Jewish tradition insists that these moments need to be public, not private. For it is not only the individual celebrants who are touched at births and weddings. These are powerful moments that also enrich the communities that come to share them. Communities need moments when they can collectively express a prevailing optimism, when they can rejoice in the continuing possibility of hope. Emile Durkheim (1858–1917), the French sociologist, once commented that communities feel robbed when couples decide to elope, for communities then lose the opportunity to express that hope, to feel that optimism.

Even rituals of grief, most notably the funeral, serve an important function for both the people in crisis as well as for those coming to lend support. Jewish funerals are hauntingly stark. Flowers are not part of traditional Jewish funerals, for they mitigate the harshness of the reality that needs to be confronted. The coffin must be wooden, so that it, like the body, will gradually return "to dust." When Jewish tradition encourages each person at the funeral to assist in the filling in of the grave, it forces each of us to confront our own mortality. The tradition reminds us that one day, we, too, will be buried in similar fashion. But while the confrontation with our own mortality can be harrowing, Jewish funerals ameliorate the inevitably profound fear by creating a sense of connectedness to other human beings. In Jewish tradition, the community does not disband at the cemetery but returns to the home of one of the relatives to gather to pray, to recollect, and to comfort. Jewish tradition insists that the mourner remain at home for seven days, to receive visitors and to be reassured that he or she is not alone. For eleven months after the death of a parent, the mourner stands in the synagogue and recites the *Kaddish*, thus acknowledging her or his need for support in the face of recent loss. Even in death, Judaism builds community and connection. It comforts us with the implicit assurance that when we die those we love will be cared for by a community similar to the one we now see assembled for someone else.

Though we will see that most Jewish rituals also have complex symbolisms, their most powerful quality may be the most obvious: they create and invigorate connections and relationships. Jewish ritual is about interrupting the pace of modern life to provide a chance to think about and to celebrate that which is more enduring, more compelling, and more important. Shabbat, births, weddings, funerals, holidays: beyond their individual significances, each helps to reestablish Jews' connections to the people who give their lives context, joy, and meaning.

RITUAL AS CONNECTION TO JEWISH LIFE

Jewish ritual plays another important role in Jewish life: it connects Jews to their tradition. It makes the spiritual odyssey that is Jewish life not an intermittent phenomenon but a regular, daily confrontation with Jewishness and with meaning.

Jewish tradition has long understood that for Judaism to play the significant emotional role in our lives that many Jews want it to, Jewish life cannot be relegated to a few important days a year or major life-cycle events. If Jewish experiences, Jewish ideas, and Jewish practices are to have any hope of shaping our dreams and spiritual quests for God, Judaism needs to be part of our ongoing sense of self. If Jewish life is to evoke passion, our senses of ourselves as Jews have to be ongoing, constant. It understands that the things people are passionate about tend to be those parts of their lives that they engage in regularly.

Jewish ritual allows passion to emerge in Jewish life by making our awareness of our Jewishness part of everyday living. Daily prayer, to which I will return in Chapter Six, is one example of such a ritual. *Kashrut*, or the Jewish system of dietary laws, is yet another. *Kashrut*, like other Jewish rituals, works on many different levels. Interestingly, the Torah does not give specific reasons for the Jewish dietary laws. While many people believe that *kashrut* was developed as a means of protecting the health of the Jews as they traversed the desert, that explanation was actually fabricated by those who wished to argue that *kashrut* was no longer relevant. *Kashrut* has much less to do with health than it does with sanctity and with connection to Judaism and the Jewish people.

There is no doubt that one function of *kashrut* is to make every act of eating a sacred act. Ritual slaughter is designed to remind us that though we are permitted to consume other animals for our own sustenance, we should be mindful of the fact that we are consuming other life to sustain our own. We may eat other animals, tradition says, but only certain animals, and only if they are slaughtered in a ritual fashion designed to be as painless as possible and to remove as much of the animal's blood as possible (the blood representing the value of the life we have taken).

Kashrut, like other Jewish eating rituals, is designed to prompt us to think about what we are eating. In an era in which fast food and "eating on the run" have become the norm, Judaism insists that it can invest eating with sanctity, perhaps even with transcendence. For a Jew who keeps kosher (eating in accordance with traditional Jewish dietary regulations), every act of eating requires decisions: Can I eat this? Which drawer (dairy or meat) do I now open? When did I last eat meat? Has it been long enough that I can now have a dairy food? These may not sound like profound questions. But because they cause us to pause, to reflect, and to appreciate each time we eat, they create regular connections to the Jewish tradition. They add sanctity to the act of eating and create brief but important moments when it becomes more likely that we may experience a sense of God's presence, and ourselves as part of a larger system of meaning and belonging.

Other Jewish rituals related to the act of eating work in the same way. Before Jews eat bread, they wash their hands in a ritual fashion, pouring water first on one hand and then on the other. They recite a blessing, and then without speaking move back to their seat, recite a blessing over bread, and then begin to eat. It is a momentary ritual, without fanfare and without the pomp and circumstance of other religious events. But it is important. Like *kashrut,* it creates a brief silence, an opportunity to feel something. In the midst of what might otherwise be a mechanical act to satisfy a purely biological need, Judaism uses ritual to create moments of holiness, brief interludes into which Jews can bring the presence of God.

Today, the single most important role for *kashrut* may be its establishing a connection between individual Jews and their people and traditions. Shabbat comes only once a week. Days inevitably go by when many people cannot find time to study. Life-cycle rituals are usually few and far between. But we eat every day, several times a day. By turning each and every act of eating into a moment that fosters awareness of our Jewishness, *kashrut* brings an element of "constancy" into Jewish life. It makes Judaism a regular part of life, and not surprisingly, in many studies, has been shown to be the single ritual that most determines the likely future Jewish identification of Jewish children. Of all factors (education, synagogue attendance, Jewish social circles, among others), it is *kashrut* that most successfully predicts how connected a Jewish child will be to Judaism when he or she reaches adulthood. There is no magic involved here. Judaism understands that commitment is born of connectedness and constancy. More than any other ritual, the dietary laws provide that daily connectedness for many Jews.

Yet even this notion of constancy does not exhaust the functions of ritual in Jewish life. Another important role that contributes to Judaism's spirituality is what we might call the "expression of wonder."

RITUAL AS THE EXPRESSION OF WONDER

Judaism recognizes that much of what many people find most spiritually moving has its roots in what we tend to call "miracles." Whether we believe that these events are miracles in the classic sense, or whether we use the word "miraculous" simply to indicate that the event is profound beyond words does not really matter. Judaism understands that there are moments in our lives that feel miraculous. Jewish ritual provides a way to express that awe and wonder, to confront the miraculous qualities of regular human life.

Almost everyone is moved by the sudden appearance of a rainbow after a summer storm. Rather than simply ignore the fragility of the rainbow and its stark contrast to the powerful thunder and lightning that often precede it, Judaism celebrates it. Upon seeing a rainbow, the tradition asserts that Jews should say a blessing: "Blessed are You, Lord our God, King of the Universe, Who remembers the Covenant, is trustworthy in His Covenant, and fulfills His promise."

This blessing is a subtle reference to Noah, to whom God said that the rainbow after the flood was a sign of God's promise never again to destroy the world. Thus, when Jews see a rainbow, the ritual of the blessing causes them to pause, to wonder, to reflect: on the fragility of the rainbow, and the fragility of human life. About the "miracle" that despite all that has happened to the planet, human life somehow survives. That in the midst of life's hectic pace, it is still possible to appreciate profound beauty.

This one simple ritual takes a moment that might otherwise pass with minimal notice and transforms it into an opportunity for awe, for wonder, for spirituality, for feeling God's presence. There are also blessings for giving birth, for lightning, for thunder, for recovery from illness; there is even a blessing to be recited upon hearing that someone has died.

Judaism celebrates the miracle in even the most mundane moments. Consider the following blessing, recited by traditional Jews after they use the bathroom:

> Praised are You, Lord our God, King of the Universe, who has fashioned human beings with wisdom and created in them many openings and many cavities. It is known and revealed before Your Throne of Glory that if one of them were to be ruptured or one of them were to be blocked, it would be impossible to survive and to

stand before You. Praised are You, God, Who heals all flesh and acts wondrously.

Many other Jewish rituals seek to sensitize Jews to the subtle but spiritually powerful qualities of nature. Shabbat begins eighteen minutes before sundown, and ends when three stars have appeared in the sky. Traditional Jews are thus keenly aware of the yearly patterns of sunset, coming earlier in the winter and then later toward summer. Rosh Ḥodesh, the beginning of the Jewish month, is tied to the appearance of the moon (now calculated mathematically). Some feminists have even suggested that the custom of a woman's going to a *mikveh* (a ritual bath) after the conclusion of her menstrual period has the capacity to evoke an awareness of nature, of the miraculous functioning of a woman's body, and of a deeply spiritual quality. Consider the following interpretation of that tradition by a leading Jewish feminist thinker:

> The mikveh simulates the original living water, the primal sea from which all life comes, the womb of the world, the amniotic tide on which the unborn child is rocked. To be reborn, one must reenter this womb and "drown" in living water. We enter the mikveh naked as an infant enters the world. . . . We emerge from the mikveh tahor [spiritually cleansed], having confronted and experienced our own death and resurrection.*

Not every ritual will touch each Jew the same way. But on the whole, we have seen that each of these brief and simple rituals is designed to make us more reflective, more sensitive to the moments in life that we all too often ignore. To many Jews, the world of Jewish ritual seems mechanical, unthinking, un-

*Rachel Adler, "Tumah and Taharah—Mikveh," in Richard Siegel, Michael and Sharon Strassfeld, *The Jewish Catalog* (Philadelphia: JPSA, 1973), p. 170.

feeling. But in reality, the tradition strives for exactly the opposite effect.

Yet the "miracles" that Jewish ritual seeks to evoke and to
celebrate are not limited to the natural world. Some are also
"miracles" in Jewish history. Hanukkah is a perfect example.
As was suggested earlier, many Jews see Hanukkah as the Jewish Christmas, or the childish celebration of a miracle they are
not even convinced took place. But here, too, the tradition
seeks not mechanical compliance but marvel, awe, and wonder at the "miracle" of Jewish history and survival.

The major ideas of Hanukkah are not complicated. The
holiday celebrates the Maccabees' recapturing of the Temple
from the Greeks, who had taken it from them and desecrated
it. According to the Talmud, the victorious Jewish troops were
intent upon restoring the Temple to its former state of purity.
But upon searching, they discovered that only one cruse of ritually pure oil remained, containing enough oil for just one day.
Making new ritually pure oil would have required eight days.
But a miracle transpired, and the small amount of oil they
found burned for the full eight days.

As we look more carefully, however, there are indications
that Hanukkah is about more than the military victory over
the Greeks and the miracle of the oil. After all, as the Talmud
notes (Shabbat 21b), if the point of the Hanukkah menorah
were to reenact the miracle of the oil, we should begin with
eight candles and count down to one. Why begin with one and
increase to eight? What is the significance of the second blessing recited upon the lighting of the candles: "Praised are You,
Lord our God, King of the Universe, Who performed miracles
for our ancestors in days of old and in our age as well"?

If we think about them carefully, the blessing and the details of the ritual suggest an answer. Hanukkah is about miracles that are still ongoing, symbolized by a growing, not a
diminishing, number of candles. Hanukkah is about not only
the victory of the Jews in their battle against the Greeks, but

about the victory of the Jewish people in their battle to survive. Hanukkah is about the miracle of Jewish existence. A small, sometimes virtually powerless people that was persecuted by ancient Greeks and Romans, medieval Christendom and Islam, and modern Nazism still survives. Many of the people who persecuted the Jews, though more numerous and more powerful than we were, are now gone. And we are here, to tell our story, to pass on our tradition. The menorah's lights are small and fragile, but they grow in number as the holiday progresses. The light shines brighter, and doesn't dim. How are we to explain this survival? Why are we still here? Is it a matter of how we have lived? God's intervention in history? Will contemporary Jewish life ensure that Jews will still be lighting the menorah, contemplating the wonder of Jewish survival, several generations from now? Does it matter if we don't survive? Why?

Hanukkah is not a Jewish Christmas. Hanukkah is about the wonder and awe of Jewish survival. It prompts us to ask ourselves, to discuss with our friends, and to explore with our children: Does Jewish existence matter? Why? What do we stand for? Would the world be missing anything if we were gone?

Yet there are still other functions for Jewish ritual. As we saw with Hanukkah, when the worlds of words and symbols unite, Jewish ritual achieves its most subtle power. Sometimes, rituals raise life's most haunting but important questions. At other times, the uniquely Jewish association between words and symbols dares us to critique the world we live in, to dream of a different world, and to commit to bringing it about.

RITUAL AS A "SUBVERSIVE" SOCIAL CRITIQUE

Many people, Jews among them, fault religion for being insufficiently critical of society and its priorities. In his famous critique of religion, Karl Marx claimed that religion was an "opiate for the masses." He said that religion fostered an unthinking sense of obedience and undermined people's ability to be critical of a system that took advantage of them. Religion, he said, had inadvertently become society's accomplice in denying their humanity.

But Marx did not understand Shabbat. He did not appreciate that beyond "imitating" God and creating connectedness to other Jews, Shabbat also has a deeply subversive quality. Throughout Jewish history, as poverty and oppression threatened to erode Jews' sense of dignity, Shabbat intervened. Virtually every detail of their Shabbat experience assured them that repair of the world was possible, and that in the interim they did matter. As the sun set, they recited the Sabbath Psalm (Psalm 92), which evoked a vision of a more just universe:

> *though the wicked sprout like grass,*
> *though all evildoers blossom,*
> *it is only that they may be destroyed forever.*
>
> *. . .*
>
> *The righteous shall blossom like a date palm,*
> *they will thrive like a cedar in Lebanon;*
> *planted in the house of the Lord,*
> *they will flourish in the courts of our God.*

On Shabbat, even the most impoverished Jews gathered around their tables, dressed in the finest clothes they had. Poor as they were, their food was more festive on Shabbat. Overworked and exhausted, they dined and they sang. In Hasidic

communities, in some to this day, they literally danced their
way out of the synagogue. At home, gathered around the table,
they danced again. They sang special Shabbat songs, known as
zemirot, such as *Menuchah ve-Simchah*, "Contentment and Joy."
Written by an unknown poet in the mid-1500s, it begins with
a standard description of Shabbat. The first verse, for example,
reads:

> *Contentment and joy, light for the Jewish people,*
> *It is a day of rest, a day of delight.*
> *Those who observe it act as witnesses*
> *That in six days, all was created and still endures.*

The next three verses continue in much the same vein. By the
fifth and final verse, however, the tone changes dramatically.
Even as the song continues to enumerate the customs of Shabbat, it suggests Jews who celebrate Shabbat are doing more
than fulfilling a biblical command. They are living a "taste of
the world to come":

> *With an additional loaf of challah and the majestic Kiddush;*
> *with delicacies aplenty and a spirit of generosity,*
> *those who revel in it will merit infinite blessing:*
> *the arrival of the Messiah, life in the world to come.*

This song and dozens of others just like it assert that Shabbat
is not only about creation, nor is it only about connection to
other people. It is about something even more cosmic. Shabbat is about a different world. It is the opportunity to experience the world repaired, humanity healed.

As Jews conclude their Shabbat meal, they begin the Grace
after Meals with a special addition, reserved primarily for
Shabbat. They add Psalm 126 to their prayer, heightening
their conviction that their present reality is not what God has
in mind for them:

When the Lord restores the fortunes of Zion
—we see it as in a dream—
our mouths shall be filled with laughter,
our tongues, with songs of joy.
. . .
They who sow in tears
shall reap with songs of joy.
Though he goes along weeping,
carrying the seed bag,
he shall come back with songs of joy
carrying his sheaves.

Thus, the myriad rituals and texts of Shabbat come not only to mimic God's rest on the seventh day, but to create an alternate reality, a taste of a world that Judaism calls *me-ein olam ha-bah*—a glimpse of a world redeemed, a vision of the messianic dream made real. Franz Rosenzweig, the German Jewish philosopher whose *Star of Redemption* became one of modern Judaism's philosophic classics, understood Shabbat in precisely this fashion. He wrote in the *Star*: "The Sabbath is the dream of perfection . . . the sign of Creation and the first revelation . . . the anticipation of redemption. . . . Indeed, on the Sabbath the congregation feels as if it were already redeemed."*

For the Jew who observes Shabbat and understands the sacred drama it creates, the message is clear. Shabbat is not about simply restricting our activity because the Torah happens to say not to work on the Sabbath (Exodus 20:10 and elsewhere); it is about living a dream, experiencing an alternative world. Jewish tradition is afraid that we will despair of the possibility of that world ever coming to be, so it creates a day on which we can actually live it. By allowing Jews to taste a bit

---

*Franz Rosenzweig, *The Star of Redemption*, tr. by William Hallo (South Bend, Ind.: University of Notre Dame Press, 1972), pp. 313–15.

of a redeemed world, Jewish life forces them to ask powerful questions about their priorities, their dreams, their willingness to make sacrifice in order to change reality. Shabbat comes not to say that everything is fine but to remind Jews that it is not and to demand that they change it.

Does the ritual "work"? For some people, it clearly does. Consider the testimonies of Jews who survived the Nazi death machine and who told of Shabbat in the camps. They spoke of inmates who violated the Nazis' law, risking immediate death by hoarding their bread from Thursday so that they could have two pieces on Friday (symbolic of the two loaves of *challah* that tradition requires on Friday evening and Shabbat afternoon). Why would people on the verge of starvation, in which Shabbat could scarcely be celebrated, take this risk? What was to be gained?

What they stood to gain was a chance to reassert their denial of Nazi Europe as an ultimate reality. Honoring Shabbat, even in a murder camp, was their way of saying, "I believe in the possibility of a better world. I deny that you are the real ruler. Despite you, I insist that I am human, that I am created in God's image, and that one day, a world will arise when good will triumph over evil, when God will triumph over you." Marx's "opiate of the masses"? Hardly. On this level, Shabbat is about rebellion, about dissatisfaction with the world, about retaining hope in the face of adversity.

To Jews today, thankfully not in the clutches of the Nazi death machine, Shabbat comes as a challenge. It is more than a taste of the world to come; it is a challenging, demanding taste, designed to recommit us in the battle to make that dream a reality. Through the unique combination of food, song, dress, and study, the fragrance of wine and the magic of fire, Jewish tradition takes a simple day and makes it profoundly spiritual. It is in ritual that Judaism's cerebral seriousness begins to give way to passion, to dreams, to a sense of the possibility of a world transformed.

As is true in poetry and music, much of what the ritual "means" is in the eye of the beholder. Not everyone will resonate to this kabbalistic (Jewish mystical) reading of Shabbat. For some, it will prove powerful. For others, it will be irrelevant, and other dimensions of Shabbat will speak more forcefully. But because Jewish rituals speak on so many different levels at the very same time, Jews of all theological and spiritual orientations can join together in celebrating them. As they do, they encourage and fuel one another's search, one another's quests for meaning and fulfillment.

Is Shabbat the only Jewish ritual that functions on so many different levels? Is it the only one that dreams of an altered world, a changed reality? Certainly not. In order to see another example of Jewish ritual speaking on many different levels, let's look at one more well-known ceremony: the Jewish wedding.

Transformation in the Jewish Wedding Ceremony

On one level, much of the wedding's imagery speaks directly to the experience of marriage and to love. The bride's circling the groom as the ceremony begins (or in some communities, the groom and bride circling each other) is a metaphor for the intertwining of the couple's lives. The *ḥuppah*, or marriage canopy, symbolizes the home they will create. The wine expresses the joy of the occasion. Even the nature of the ring has symbolic significance. While the ring may be decorated, the decorations are not supposed to be cut out of the ring, for the circularity and solidity of the metal suggest the permanence of the relationship now being created.

On this level alone, the wedding ceremony is very powerful. It uses symbolism to highlight and to make explicit what most of the people assembled are already feeling. By using distinctly

Jewish symbols, the wedding channels the power of the moment—the senses of love, hope, and gratitude that prevail—
and creates a passionate Jewish experience tied to community
and to tradition.

But as was true in the case of Shabbat, the power and spiritual richness of Jewish tradition become even more apparent
when the wedding's symbols combine with liturgy, with the
power of words. Toward the end of the ceremony, the officiant
recites a group of blessings known as the *Sheva Berakhot*, the
"Seven Blessings." As with Shabbat, these blessings do more
than speak about the event at hand; they invite the community assembled to imagine a utopian, more perfected world. At
first blush, the blessings are quite simple. They read:

1. Praised are You, O Lord our God, King of the Universe, Creator of the fruit of the vine.
2. Praised are You, O Lord our God, King of the Universe, who created all things for Your glory.
3. Praised are You, O Lord our God, King of the Universe, Creator of man.
4. Praised are You, O Lord our God, King of the Universe, who created man and woman in Your image,
   fashioning woman from man as his mate, that together they might perpetuate life. Praised are You,
   O Lord, Creator of man.
5. May Zion rejoice as her children are restored to her
   in joy. Praised are You, O Lord, who causes Zion to
   rejoice at her children's return.
6. Grant perfect joy to these loving companions, as
   You did to the first man and woman in the Garden
   of Eden. Praised are You, O Lord, who grants the
   joy of bride and groom.
7. Praised are You, O Lord our God, King of the Universe, who created joy and gladness, bride and
   groom, mirth, song, delight and rejoicing, love and

harmony, peace and companionship. O Lord our God, may there ever be heard in the cities of Judah and in the streets of Jerusalem voices of joy and gladness, voices of bride and groom, the jubilant voices of those joined in marriage under the bridal canopy, the voices of young people feasting and singing. Praised are You, O Lord, who causes the groom to rejoice with his bride.

What is striking about these blessings is that they scarcely mention love, and mention marriage only in the last blessing. Instead of love and marriage, the blessings focus on God's creation of the world (blessings 2, 3, and 4), the Garden of Eden (blessing 6), and Jerusalem, or Zion (blessing 5)! Why? What is the liturgy trying to say by importing these images into the center of the wedding ceremony?

This is another example of Jewish ritual "transporting" its participants to a wholly different place and time. Judaism suggests that the profundity and purity of human commitment implied by a wedding make it possible to believe in a fully transformed, healed world. The bride and groom, the *Sheva Berakhot* seem to imply, are not simply the two people of flesh and blood getting married. They are the perfected, idealized loving companions, Adam and Eve in the Garden of Eden. The purity of their love rekindles our dream of a wholly pure existence, the Garden of Eden. Jewish tradition asserts that their commitment to each other furthers God's process of creation, bringing the world one step closer to its eventual perfection. The bride and groom are also the young men and women of a rebuilt Jerusalem, whose love bespeaks perfection, salvation, redemption of the Jewish people, and, ultimately, the world.

Though when we are at a wedding we are often focused on the people involved and the moment at hand, the richness of this Jewish ritual—symbolism combined with liturgy—seeks to transport us, even momentarily, to a very different time and place. If we allow it to, the wedding—like Shabbat—transforms us and places us in a transformed world, challenging us, in turn, to use our energies to create it.

But the specifics are less important than the overall point; when we appreciate the subtle allusions and liturgical references of Jewish ritual, we begin to see that part of the power of ritual is in its ability to transport us figuratively to a different place and time, where we participate however metaphorically in a world transformed, in a reality healed, in life as we wish it could be. Regardless of our theologies or our particular struggles with faith, we taste something different, something better, and we emerge invigorated, touched, and spiritually enriched.

RITUAL AS THE SETTING FOR COMMUNAL INTROSPECTION

While Jewish ritual makes use of many different symbols such as wine, *ḥuppah*, *tallit* (prayer shawl), the shattering of a glass, Seder plates, and the like, we have begun to notice that it is ultimately words that give Jewish rituals not only their distinctly Jewish quality but much of their power. Yet words do more than add texture to ritual, more even than make the rituals distinctly Jewish. Words give Jewish rituals their intellectual profundity. As an example, let's consider the *bris*.

Like other rituals, the *bris* (the ritual circumcision of a boy on his eighth day of life) works on several levels. On the surface, it involves two stages: the actual circumcision and the naming of the child. Slightly below that surface, the liturgy portrays the event as an important link in the chain of the Jewish people, making explicit reference to God's command that Abraham circumcise Isaac. As all the assembled express the wish that "just as he has been brought into the covenant, so may he . . . stand under the marriage canopy," they express their hope that he will know love (alluded to by the "marriage canopy" image), and that he, too, will become part of the chain. By obliging parents to circumcise their son, the tradition reminds them that he is their responsibility but ultimately not their possession. Important as he is to his family, he is needed for something bigger, something grander, something that stretches across generations and continents.

But the *bris* also has a deeply contemplative side. It raises haunting, even painful questions not readily apparent until we look closely at the liturgy. Below the surface of its symbolism, the *bris* conveys Judaism's sense that even life's most joyous moments can be opportunities for confronting who we are, for examining closely the ways in which we live our lives. In order to find this more meditative, almost ominous, side of the *bris*, we need to look very closely at its liturgy and the questions those texts raise.

As the *bris* begins, the *mohel* recites a biblical selection that seems wholly inappropriate to the occasion. The passage reads as follows:

> The Lord spoke to Moses, saying, "Phinehas, son of Eleazar son of Aaron the priest, has turned back My wrath from the Israelites by displaying among them his passion for Me, so that I did not wipe out the Israelite people in My passion. Say, therefore, 'I grant him My pact of peace.'"
>
> (NUMBERS 25:10–12)

Who is this Phinehas, and why is he mentioned in the *bris*? The ceremony never mentions him again, nor does it offer an explanation. But as we turn to the Torah and read the section that precedes these verses, hints begin to emerge. The Torah explains that Phinehas had demonstrated zealousness for God, passion for God's place in Israelite life. According to the Torah (Numbers 25:1–8), while the Israelites were in the desert, some attached themselves to Moabite women and sacrificed to the Moabite gods. God commanded Moses to slay the people responsible, and just as Moses was gathering the people, one of the Israelites purposely brought in his Midianite woman "companion." When Phinehas, son of Eleazar son of Aaron the priest, saw this, he left the assembly and, taking a spear in his hand, he followed the Israelite into the chamber and stabbed both the Israelite and the woman, killing them.

By deftly alluding to this very painful passage, then, the *bris* ceremony subtly introduces the whole question of passionate devotion to the Jewish community. Jewish tradition recognizes that there are very few parents for whom the *bris* is not an anxious moment. No matter how committed they may be to performing this tradition, there is something difficult about watching even a minor surgical procedure on a newborn baby. The community in attendance often feels this tension, too. But rather than ignore the tension, or vitiate it as some *mohalim* (plural of *mohel*) do by using humor, Jewish tradition capitalizes on the tension and this parental expression of devotion. It reminds us of Phinehas, and effectively asks: How much are we willing to do for causes that are important to us? What in life is so sacred to us that we would risk all for it? Which causes are so important to us that we will let no one stand in their way? As we formally welcome a new child to the Jewish community, are we going to transmit those passions to him? Will this child witness that passion? When? How?

Had it been less wise, Jewish tradition might have sought to raise these issues in some other way. It could have instructed parents and families to study the passages about Phinehas on the occasion of the child's birth. But the power of ritual, and indeed of Jewish life, is that it burrows deeper into the soul than any merely intellectual enterprise. It touches people more profoundly than any sermon could. The presence of the child, frail and sometimes crying, evokes the frailty of the Jewish people. Parents and family at the moment of the *bris* are deeply devoted to protecting the child and to nurturing him; but "What about the Jewish community?" the *bris* seems to ask. Will we protect that as passionately?

Yet even these questions do not exhaust the profundity of the *bris*. The verses from Numbers 25 about the Midianite woman whom Phinehas killed recall a moment later in the very same chapter when God commands Moses to attack and defeat the Midianites for their having lured Israelites away from God. That command might seem uninteresting, but suddenly, we recall that Moses' wife was a Midianite! Indeed, her father is described as "Jethro, the Priest of Midian" (Exodus 18:1).

Moses does not respond to the command to attack the Midianites. He seems to ignore it, forcing God to remind him later in the book. Is that because Moses cannot bear the thought of attacking a people one of whose members he had married? Is the *bris* ceremony, as a new child is ushered not only into a community but into a family as well, reminding us of how fragile a family can be? Is Jewish tradition, in addition to everything else that is going on at that moment, also encouraging us to think about the competing loyalties that family often involves? Does the ritual of the *bris* try to focus our attention on the profound investments we have to make to keep our families together?

Perhaps. Because ritual is in many senses somewhat like poetry, the *bris* speaks to different people in different ways. There is no one "correct" way to interpret the *bris*. But what is clear is that there is great subtlety and depth to this ritual. As we learn more about the texts of the ritual and the other Jewish themes to which they allude, our associations with the *bris* become ever more profound. "The greater the learning, the greater the reward," suggests the Mishnah (Avot 5:22). When Jewish rituals sometimes fail to speak to modern Jews it is largely because many Jews have never been exposed to the subtle but powerful suggestions behind each of these sacred dramas.

Many Jews today have not been taught the texts that are the foundations of these rituals. But it can all be learned. What is difficult for many modern Jews to accept is that beginning the Jewish spiritual journey will require learning about Jewish tradition and culture. But that is not as daunting a challenge as it might seem. I'll return to how to begin that process in Chapter Eight.

DOES RITUAL ALWAYS "WORK"?

Having examined briefly several of the ways in which ritual seeks to enrich the spirituality of Jewish life, an important question arises: "Does it work?" Will participation in Jewish rituals have the impact described in these pages? Will I be touched? Will they move me?

These are difficult questions to answer, since much of what ritual touches is primal, so deeply personal. To a great extent, our response to ritual will depend more on our emotional, intellectual, and psychological makeup than it will on the ceremony itself.

But what Jewish life has to offer is a way of life that speaks to many different people in varying ways, precisely because its rituals operate on many different levels. Jewish tradition recognizes that many of the most powerful times of our lives are moments of wonder, of profound gratitude, of fear. They are moments when we dare to dream: of who we could be, of what the world could become. The ritual of Jewish life is about all this, and more. What makes Jewish ritual so powerful is its combination of symbol with word, and the many potential levels of meaning that emerge from that partnership. Jewish life is about celebrating life's most momentous occasions, but also about transforming the mundane. It is about asking probing questions, but also about building relationships with the people who most enrich our lives.

Judaism knows that rituals do, at times, become stale. It is possible to perform a ceremony so often that it becomes rote. That is one of the reasons that Judaism places community at the center of ritual. The tradition hopes that if ritual life stops touching us, the presence of community can add power and inspiration, supplementing our experience with the insights and faith of others. And that is also why each generation of Jews alters rituals slightly, sometimes creating new ones and finding new meaning for old traditions. The American Jewish community has probably been more creative in this respect than any other Jewish community in history. American Jewish life has created the *simhat bat* ceremony for naming girls and for bringing them into the covenant. Jewish women have created ceremonies for the onset of menstruation as well as for menopause. For those seeking the richness of Jewish life through ritual, there has never been a Jewish community that had more to offer.

Regardless of how it functions for each individual, however, ritual is key to Judaism's spirituality. On one level, ritual is the balance to Judaism's emphasis on study. Though Jews study with partners, *talmud torah* is still more individual than it is communal. Study, though a passionate experience in many ways, essentially provides a deeply intellectual experience. It challenges our minds, and in so doing reasserts Judaism's commitment to intellectual openness and honesty.

Ritual, in turn, provides much of the emotion of Jewish life. The holiday of *Simhat Torah* transforms the study of Torah from an intellectual experience to a communal expression of joy, celebration, and renewal. The first night of Shavuot, when traditional Jews stay awake studying until the sun rises in order to demonstrate their love of learning, evokes a different kind of power. As they walk from one study session to another, through neighborhoods that are completely still and asleep, being awake in the middle of the night conveys a sense of communal devotion to what during much of the year is more personal and individual. There is an eerie power to the quiet of the night that no intellectual experience can match. The slightly overwhelming feeling of the night and the darkness of the sky remind us that being Jewish is about being part of something more majestic and magisterial than we are. Being Jewish, and participating in Jewish ritual in particular, are about experiencing the transcendent, about creating moments so powerful that we emerge feeling that we have experienced the closeness of God.

But on another level, study and ritual are inseparable. There is a ritual quality to the ways that Jews study; it is text that gives ritual its distinctive quality. United, study and ritual seek to create those moments where, even for skeptics, God's presence emerges, where Judaism addresses issues of ultimate significance, where Jewish life begins to touch the nerves that define and shape our humanity. Jewish ritual does not demand that we believe; the rituals we've examined did not require that we utter statements of absolute faith. On the contrary: Jewish ritual tries to make it possible for us to have faith. In Jewish life, ritual is not just what we do when we have come to a place of faith and spirituality; it is part of Judaism's road to those feelings. For those Jews who want to be touched by the power of Jewish life, ritual is one of the important roads to explore.

---◆---

CHAPTER FIVE

MITZVAH AS COMMANDMENT— COMMITMENT AND THE ROAD TO SPIRITUALITY

---◆---

JEWISH TRADITION FOSTERS SPIRITUALITY BY CREAT-
ing feelings of transcendence, the sense that we are part of
something infinite, much larger than ourselves in a variety of
ways. Judaism's encounter with sacred texts nurtures spirituality by including Jews in a timeless conversation that began
long ago and that touches on ultimate questions about the
meaning of human life. Ritual, the second step to spirituality
that I discussed, operates in much the same way. Though ritual
is not nearly as cerebral as study, it also creates connections—

to other Jews, to a sense of mystery and grandeur, to God. The discussion of ritual in the previous chapter leads naturally to a third crucial Jewish road to God, a road I will call *mitzvah*.

In the American lexicon, the word *mitzvah* is commonly misunderstood to mean "good deed." It's a *mitzvah*, people say, to care for the sick, to give charity. Doing a *mitzvah*, popular culture suggests, is to do something "nice." But the Hebrew word *mitzvah* means neither "good deed" nor "nice." It means "commandment." "Doing a *mitzvah*" might well be nice, but—perhaps surprisingly—Judaism values it not only for its "kindness" but for its "commandedness" as well.

Mitzvah is often an extraordinarily difficult concept for modern Jews. Many Jews resist what they see as Judaism's tendency to regulate too many elements of life. They have trouble understanding why a religious tradition tells them what to eat, what to wear, what percentage of their income to give to charity, and when and how to pray, whom they can marry, and even when and how to make love. Why not strive for some abstract morality, without so many seemingly unnecessary regulations? As some people cleverly phrase the question, "Considering how desperately the world needs kind and caring people, does God really care about the details?"

Yet as much as it sounds reasonable to wonder whether God really cares about the details, these specific elements of Jewish life are often important not necessarily because God cares about them, but because we need them. It is through our attention to detail, tradition claims, that we express what Judaism calls a sense of "commandedness," a sense that we behave in a certain way in order to construct a relationship with God. *Mitzvah* is designed not to make unnecessary limitations on our privacy and autonomy, but to express the idea that if we wish to feel God's presence, we need to evoke that feeling in action. We need to behave as if we had a real relationship with God; *mitzvah*, therefore, is one of Judaism's most important roads to spiritual fulfillment.

Jews today are understandably resistant to the many implications of *mitzvah*. The very notion of commandedness is not
only at odds with the pervasive message of American culture,
but it is also one of the elements of Jewish life about which
Jews hear the least. Because it is unfamiliar, it is one of the
parts of Jewish life that sounds most strange.

Mitzvah as commandedness seems much more foreign than
many of the other elements of Jewish life that we have examined thus far. Difficult as faith in God can be, we expect at the
outset that a spiritual encounter with our religious tradition
will mean exploring the issue of God. Even if we have had no
experience with Jewish texts, we somehow know that those
books exist, and we are not surprised to learn how important
they are. We may not know a tremendous amount about Judaism's view of God, the nature of Jewish texts, or the details
of Jewish ritual, but we are not surprised to find that they are
parts of the Jewish journey to spirituality.

That is not the case with *mitzvah*. In *mitzvah*, we encounter
part of our tradition without parallel in Western culture. It is a
part of Judaism many Jews have never heard of or seriously
considered as a viable element of their own spiritual lives. It
also flies in the face of our secular emphasis on autonomy and
independence.

Jews today therefore ask a variety of important questions:
Why is commandedness so central to Jews' quest for spirituality?
How does the concept of *mitzvah* contribute to our formulating
a sophisticated response to the ubiquitous question "Why be
Jewish?" Is it really so central to Judaism and Jewish spirituality?

THE PLACE OF *MITZVAH* IN JEWISH TRADITION

As difficult as the notion of commandedness is, as strange as
mitzvah sounds, even a cursory reading of the Jewish tradition

reveals that this concept has long been central to Judaism and Jewish life. Indeed, *mitzvah* is one of Judaism's most important roads to spirituality.

How do we know that *mitzvah* is so central to Jewish life? There are many important indications. Consider, for example, many of the rituals discussed in the previous chapter. Almost every one of them—kindling Sabbath candles, lighting the Hanukkah menorah, attending a *bris*, a conversion, a wedding, a Passover Seder—is accompanied by a simple but virtually omnipresent Jewish liturgical formula. The central idea of that formula is commandment. It begins, "Praised are You, Lord our God, Ruler of the Universe." The formula then continues, *asher kiddeshanu be-mitzvotav ve-tzivvanu*, which means "who has sanctified us with *commandments*, and has *commanded us* to . . ." This wording suggests the fundamental Jewish claim that sanctity, or sensing God's presence, depends in large part on the ideal of commandedness, of *mitzvah*.

Nor is the formula of the traditional blessing the only indication that Judaism considers *mitzvah* a crucial tool in the pursuit of spirituality. This idea is apparent in biblical and rabbinic literature as well. Let's consider a few of the most important examples.

Mitzvah—the Jewish emphasis on commanded behavior—appears as early as the creation story. In the very first chapter of the Bible, God creates Adam and Eve and commands them: "Be fruitful and multiply, fill the earth and master it" (Genesis 1:28). Almost immediately thereafter, God again commands both Adam and Eve, "Of every tree of the garden you are free to eat, but as for the tree of knowledge of good and bad, you must not eat of it" (Genesis 2:16–17). The Torah's point is clear: even in the very first encounters between God and human beings, God's demand—command, or *mitzvah*—is central.

The Torah continues to allude to the importance of command even after creation. Shortly after completing the world,

God surveys creation and finds it utterly and hopelessly sinful. God decides to destroy humanity, and tells a man named Noah that he and his family will be the progenitors of a new generation of human beings. God tells Noah to build an ark in which his family and various animal species can ride out the storm that will destroy all other living things. Noah complies, and for forty days and forty nights the ark is tossed about by the turbulent waters raging over the earth.

When the waters finally recede and Noah and his family exit the ark onto Mount Ararat, God speaks to them and says:

> Every creature that lives shall be yours to eat. . . . You must not, however, eat flesh with its life blood in it. . . . Whoever sheds the blood of man, by man shall his blood be shed. . . . Be fertile, then, and increase; abound on the earth and increase on it.
>
> (GENESIS 9:3–7)

Here, too, it is command—not some nebulous exhortation to be kind—that is the central feature of God's relationship to people.

This emphasis on command continues throughout the Torah. Early in God's relationship with Abraham, God commands him to circumcise his son Isaac. God offers no rational explanation for this command, but Abraham, the Jews' earliest model of faith, accepts the command and performs it. Centuries later, as Moses leads the Israelites out of Egypt, God immediately directs the People to Mount Sinai, the place where God will reveal Torah—most commonly represented by what we commonly call the Ten *Commandments*. The word "Torah," in fact, means "law." To receive the Torah, Jewish tradition claims, is to receive the Law. To hear God's revelation— to be in relationship with God, Judaism insists—is to hear how God commands human beings to behave. To live a life of spiritual moment is to live with our autonomy partially curtailed in order that we keep in mind our relationship with a Force beyond us.

The importance of *mitzvah* in Jewish life emerges most clearly in an astonishing statement that the Talmud repeats three times. In the name of Rabbi Ḥaninah, an important Talmudic authority, the Talmud declares (Bava Kamma 87a): "Greater is the one who is commanded to perform a deed and does so, than one who is not commanded to perform that deed but does it."

This statement seems astonishing because American culture sees the world differently. Modern secularism tends to value the spirit of volunteerism—people who give of their time, their money, and their energy of their own accord. What makes those actions laudatory, in American society, is the person's decision to act in such a giving fashion even though the action was not required.

But whereas secular culture seems to value actions performed out of choice, the Talmud demonstrates that Jewish tradition sees the world differently. Rabbi Ḥaninah asserts (and no one in the entire Talmud disputes him) that actions performed of our own volition may be honorable, but that it is still preferable to act in response to *command*.

Rabbi Ḥaninah's claim seems counterintuitive. Commandedness, in some ways, seems to undermine what most Jews want from their spiritual odysseys. Many Jews today believe that spirituality should provide an escape from the rigors and pressures of the world they normally occupy. Spirituality, they believe, should offer some respite from the endless responsibilities that call upon them. Why would they possibly want religion to add to the list of "shoulds" in their lives? Why does Rabbi Ḥaninah assert that it is better to act out of command than choice?

In the following pages, we will examine several different messages that *mitzvah* conveys; we'll encounter several reasons that Jewish tradition has always seen *mitzvah* as such a powerful spiritual tool. I will argue that *mitzvah* does contribute to a life rich with feelings of transcendence and encounters with ultimate meaning. The world of *mitzvah* requires that we think about Jewish life differently than we have in the past. But *mitzvah* is also key to recapturing the elusive spiritual power that many Jews want and that they deeply believe Judaism can still provide.

THE FIRST FUNCTION OF MITZVAH: COMMANDMENT AS SPIRITUAL DISCIPLINE

One of the most important reasons for Judaism's emphasis on *mitzvah* is what one might call "spiritual discipline." Recall Mordecai Kaplan's three Bs discussed in Chapter Two. Kaplan suggested that Jews ought to conceptualize their encounter with Jewish life in terms of believing, behaving, and belonging. In contradistinction to much of modern culture, Jewish tradition claims that behavior—and not belief—may be the most important point of entry, for behaving can ultimately lead to believing. Discipline, Judaism asserts, has the capacity to profoundly alter how we feel. *Mitzvah* is its way of affording that discipline.

Is this reading of *mitzvah* an authentic component of traditional Judaism, or is it a modern "rewrite" of an old theological concept? This is an important question, for throughout this book, I have been making an argument for a traditional reading of Jewish life as filled with spiritual richness and potential. Thus it is necessary to clarify the degree to which this reading is a fair representation of traditional Jewish perspectives on *mitzvah*.

Before the modern era, few Jews explored the functional or psychological explanations of *mitzvah*. Jews had a clear theological basis for their concentration on commandments—they believed that God revealed not only the Torah but the entire system of Jewish law. They believed without question that God expected Jews to observe the commandments. As a result, the psychosocial functions of *mitzvah* did not seem particularly important. Theology and the socioeconomic pressure to conform in Jewish communities of old were so powerful that for many Jews there was simply no question about the centrality of *mitzvah* in their lives.

But Jews today live in a more complicated theological environment. The certitude about God and commandments that characterized Jewish communities in years gone by eludes many searching Jews today. With the impact of theology receding in many Jews' personal lives, a greater interest in psychological and social roles for *mitzvah* has developed.

Nonetheless, these interests are not as new as they might seem. If we look carefully at traditional Jewish sources, we do find evidence of an awareness of a psychological function for *mitzvah*, even in the highly theologically charged communities of the Middle Ages.

Recall the comment of Rabbi Ḥaninah, who declared: "Greater is the one who is commanded to perform a deed and does so, than one who is not commanded to perform that deed but does it." The Talmud cites his comment on three different occasions, each time in exactly the same language. On one of those occasions, the Tosafot, perhaps the most important medieval Jewish commentators on the Talmud, say nothing at all. But in response to the other two (identical) citations, they offer very different comments. One reflects classic Jewish theology. Why is one who is commanded and performs the action considered greater? Because, say the Tosafot:

> he is constantly attentive to [his need to] subjugate his desires [to the requirements of the commandments] and to perform the commandments of his Creator.
>
> (TOSAFOT AVODAH ZARAH 3A S.V. *gadol*)

This seems to be the relatively standard Jewish theological position we summarized earlier: God has commanded, and a person who performs an action in response to God is rewarded even more.

But this is not the only explanation of *mitzvah* that the Tosafot present in their commentaries in the Talmud. In reaction to another instance of Rabbi Ḥaninah's famous claim, the Tosafot offer a much more psychologically based explanation for *mitzvah*. Implicitly, they suggest that building a relationship with God is not unlike building and maintaining relationships with other human beings. If loving another human being sometimes means taking concrete steps to renew and to express feelings of love, Judaism says that Jews need to do the same with God. If we know that with people—with whom we share dinner tables, houses, and beds—feelings of distance inevitably arise, that will happen no less with God. If in human relationships it is essential to act to maintain love and connectedness, Judaism suggests that surely our even more difficult relationships with God will require action if they are to matter. *Mitzvah*, the Tosafot suggest, is the "action" that Judaism provides to maintain the relationship. Consider their other commentary on Rabbi Ḥaninah:

> It appears that this is the reason that someone who is commanded and acts is preferable: for he is worried and preoccupied that he will transgress more than someone who is not commanded, who is as if he [has all his yearnings and needs satisfied, and can ignore them whenever he wishes].
>
> (TOSAFOT KIDDUSHIN 31A S.V. *gadol*)

While this explanation seems less "classically theological" than the first, the argument of the Tosafot here is important. Their commentary on Rabbi Ḥaninah suggests that Judaism's commandedness and the discipline it implies create a constancy of awareness. Without commandments, they suggest, we are like those who have no needs. But with commandments, we become like those who are hungry, constantly seeking sources of food, ways to satisfy our appetites. People who are hungry, the Tosafot suggest, are always aware of their need for food. Similarly, they claim, Jews who feel commanded by *mitzvot* (the Hebrew plural for *mitzvah*) have a heightened spiritual awareness. The Tosafot suggest that, ultimately, the discipline of *mitzvah* creates an appetite for spiritual sensitivity that Judaism cannot otherwise provide.

Jewish life contends that if Jews are serious about searching for God's closeness, for spirituality, then we have to undertake a serious commitment to the behaviors that can make that possible. Many of the specific elements of those behaviors are the rituals discussed in the previous chapter. But it is the backdrop of *mitzvah*, of discipline and obligation, that makes it more likely that rituals will be celebrated. Thus, it is *mitzvah* that gives them texture and context, ensuring that in addition to being lovely ethnic celebrations, they will nurture and further our quests for transcendence.

Note that the approach of the Tosafot to *mitzvah* does not require any particular theological explanation for where commandments come from or Who revealed them. This commentary on Rabbi Ḥaninah does not even mention God, a Creator or Commander. Theology is effectively absent here. While theological issues surrounding the commandments are crucial questions, issues that in many respects animate the conflict between today's various Jewish denominations, the Tosafot themselves imply that Jews questing for spirituality do not always need to confront those questions right away. As seriously as many Jewish communities take their theologies of commandment, the importance of *mitzvah* on spiritual journeys is not exclusively theological. It is also related to the Jews' quest for "relationship with God."

Mitzvah, their second interpretation suggests, makes a simple psychological claim: if Judaism's quest for spirituality is a process of working slowly toward a "relationship with God," then the daily content of Jewish life has to reflect that. With other human beings, building and maintaining relationships requires the commitment of regular behaviors. Though we rarely use such terminology, maintaining human relationships involves commandedness. Judaism suggests that relationship with God requires no less.

Many dimensions of Jewish tradition assert that we can learn a great deal about spiritual possibilities and relationships with God from relationships with other people. The tradition recognizes that these two sorts of relationships are certainly not identical, but it sees relationships with people as the closest that we can come to imagining a relationship with God. For that reason, for example, the rabbis of the Talmudic period read the Song of Songs, a rather graphic biblical love poem, as a metaphor for God's love for Israel, for Jews' relationship with God. But the tradition's analogy between relationships with God and relationships with other people was not limited to the love reflected in the Song of Songs. Consider once again the Tosafot's commentary on Rabbi Ḥaninah, and note how deftly it makes the same point:

> It appears that this is the reason that someone who is commanded and acts is preferable: for he is worried and preoccupied that he will transgress more than someone who is not commanded, who is as if he [has all his yearnings and needs satisfied, and can ignore them whenever he wishes].

While this psychological explanation of *mitzvah*, with its analogy of human relationships to a quest for God, may seem highly theoretical, the sociology of the modern American Jewish community suggests that *mitzvah* in this sense still functions well today. *Mitzvah* has proven itself to be the element of Jewish life that characterizes the most vibrant and successful Jewish communities. In traditional communities that take the notion of *mitzvah* seriously, Jews have built this concept into their lives and often feel a connection to the cosmic, to the universe beyond them. Theirs are the Jewish communities in which ritual is regular, in which study pervades communal and family life, in which Jewish life is passionate life. Their children are the ones for whom Jewishness is as basic and central as their gender. These Jewish communities do not all look alike; indeed, they live the notion of *mitzvah* in sometimes radically different ways. But *mitzvah* as a sense of spiritual discipline pervades them all, and the results are clear. The Tosafists' insight that commandedness creates devotion, intensity, and, ultimately, spirituality, is no less true today than it ever was before.

Yet despite all the evidence that the devotion implied by commandedness does work, that it does evoke the spirituality that modern Jews claim to want, it is very common for Jews today to resist the idea of *mitzvah*. Many Jews much prefer to speak of Jewish life as a commitment to certain ethics or values, rather than entertain the idea that there is a necessary rigor to Judaism's spiritual richness. Why? Because as they come to understand the concept of *mitzvah*, Jews realize that a serious encounter with this element of Jewish life will inevitably place some constraints on their autonomy. But in many nonreligious spheres of life, modern Jews and non-Jews do, in fact, make connections between discipline and spirituality. Indeed, there is an irony in American Jews' common dismissal of discipline as an avenue to spirituality, precisely because Americans—Jews and non-Jews alike—often take discipline very seriously. They understand that when they want to add to their lives a quality of meaning, of seeking purpose, of commitment to some "higher" enterprise, they need to express that quest in behaviors that are regular and ongoing. They understand that the commitment to those behaviors both represents their new search, and actually deepens and intensifies it.

Many of the activities that modern Americans take on as they search for meaning or a sense of purpose are not overtly religious. Yet these actions often take on a "spiritual" quality because they help the people who commit to them move away from their normal, daily preoccupations. These behaviors help people carve out a place in their lives where their minds can roam, where their spirits can soar, where they can point with satisfaction to focusing on goals and commitments that tie them to a larger scheme of things, a grander, richer vision of the universe. These behaviors often take on the quality of "spiritual discipline" because their regularity implies a seriousness of purpose that is deeply satisfying, sometimes because it cuts against the grain of what society seems to suggest is important.

Consider a few examples of how such activities become "spiritual discipline" for modern Americans. For serious musicians, regular practice does more than improve their skills. Musicians' commitment to time with their instrument—a commitment that they are reluctant to violate—evokes a seriousness of purpose, a sense of direction, even a quality of sanctity about the role of music in their lives. For musicians to whom playing an instrument genuinely "speaks," practice is about more than perfecting technique. It is about those moments when they forget that they are practicing, when their minds wander and seem to touch a part of the world where only what is genuinely important seems to matter, where the day-to-day details of life fade into the background. For such people, practicing regularly is one way of reminding themselves of how important those feelings are to them; the intensity and rigor of their practice schedule communicates a seriousness about the enterprise, and creates the sort of intensity that makes that almost "magical" feeling possible.

For other people, this sort of discipline and its occasionally spiritual qualities emerge more clearly in athletic pursuits. Here as well, the reason many people refuse to skip a workout or take a day off from running has less to do with regression in their physical condition than it does with a loss of psychological momentum that has become important to them. Working out according to a fixed schedule is their way of saying that this is an important part of their life. It is their way of reminding themselves that life often becomes so busy that they fail to take care of themselves. To insist on a workout, even in the face of a terribly busy schedule, is to insist that creating those moments when their minds can roam and wander is an important dimension of their lives. Something happens to them when they run or cycle or swim; doing it regularly expresses a seriousness about that pursuit, and that seriousness only heightens the intensity of the feelings that sometimes accompany the activity.

Mitzvah is the way that Judaism communicates that sense of sanctity and psychological momentum about Jewish spiritual life. It is the tool that Judaism uses to say that the feelings that come from sensing God's closeness cannot be left to chance or luck. Like the feelings that sometimes come from playing a Mozart sonata, the intimacy, comfort, and security that often accompany religious experience have to be nurtured. They require a statement that we are genuinely committed to this relationship, that God's presence is something for which we are willing to work. *Mitzvah* is the discipline Jews use to say that these feelings matter, that Judaism and what it can provide are important. The discipline of *mitzvah* and the intensity that emerges from it are what Jews use to create spirituality.

Sadly, because the Jewish education that many modern Jews received often concentrated on "hows" and "musts" without explaining the "whys," many American Jews today are convinced that the rigors of Jewish life are the last place to search for spirituality. Consider the following irony: while Jews today often find *kashrut* (Judaism's system of dietary restrictions) onerous and old-fashioned, they frequently begin their searches for purpose and for transcendent meaning (searches that I have been calling "spiritual odysseys") by committing to vegetarianism in highly disciplined ways. It is not discipline that many

Jews find problematic; it is discipline within Judaism.

This observation is not meant to diminish the importance of discipline in the arts, athletics, or other moral systems. Precisely the opposite is the case. These examples of discipline in modern American society demonstrate that the quest for meaning in modern life often requires discipline. The question that spiritually questing Jews have to ask themselves is which set of disciplines they will build into their lives. If Judaism is to mean something, both tradition and modern sociology suggest that discipline has to be part of Jewish life. That is the role of *mitzvah*. How to begin is a subject I'll discuss in Chapter Eight.

A SECOND FUNCTION OF MITZVAH: COMMANDMENT AS AN EXPRESSION OF SUBMISSION

Thus far, I have pointed primarily to a psychological reading of *mitzvah*, which focused more on Jews' emotional needs and reactions than it did on God. However, an examination of the traditional view of *mitzvah* would be sorely lacking if it did not attend to a slightly different reading of commandments, in which God plays a much more overt role.

While the discussion of discipline in religious life emphasized the second explanation of Rabbi Ḥaninah offered by the Tosafot, we should not ignore their first comment. In that passage, they write that a focus on *mitzvah* makes a person

> constantly attentive to [his need to] subjugate his desires [to the requirements of the commandments] and to perform the commandments of his Creator.

Here, the Tosafot seem to be suggesting that another crucial dimension of Jewish spirituality is what we might call spiritual humility, or submission.

What is the difference between discipline and submission? For our discussion, I'll suggest that discipline focuses on the needs of the individual Jew, while humility focuses on our relationship to something else, a Being beyond us. Discipline focuses on our needs, while submission focuses on the demands of God.

It is important that we note that this message about *mitzvah* is in some ways at odds with the various explanations of ritual offered in the previous chapter. The notion of submission argues that the importance of the rituals, beyond whatever psychological, intellectual, or moral import they may convey, lies in the fact that they are commanded, and that in their commandedness, they remind us of our place vis-à-vis God. Taken to its extreme, this notion argues that the importance of the commanded rituals is not their creating holiness, community, or opportunities for introspection, but simply in their being commanded. No one has articulated this idea more forcefully than the modern Israeli philosopher Yeshayahu Leibowitz (1903–1994). Leibowitz, who makes the case more strongly than most people are willing to, goes so far as to suggest:

> Every reason given for the *mitzvot* which bases itself on human needs from any consideration of the concept of need, whether intellectual, ethical, social, national—voids the *mitzvot* from every religious meaning. If they are meant to benefit society or if they maintain the Jewish people, then he who performs them does not serve God but himself, or society or his people. In any case, he does not serve God but uses the Torah of God for his benefit and as a means to satisfy his needs. The reason for the *mitzvot* is the worship of God.[*]

[*]Cited in David Hartman, *A Living Covenant: The Living Spirit in Traditional Judaism* (New York: The Free Press, 1985), p. 111.

Though few other Jews are willing to put the case as starkly as Leibowitz, we have seen that his position has important traditional roots. Even the Tosafot suggest that submission is important in its own right. Again, because that notion seems so counterintuitive, an analogy to explain the spiritual power of submission may help. Why is submission, or spiritual humility, such an important part of Jewish life? Our responses to nature serve as one indication.

Nature's grandeur—a sunset or waterfall, the desolate vastness of the desert, or the imperious glory of a mountain range—communicates a sense of transcendence as nothing else can. Why is that? Why do so many people respond to nature this way? What is it about nature that enables people to feel God's presence? Part of what is powerful about nature is the sheer magnitude of its phenomena. Something about the immensity and the power of those phenomena makes us feel small, somehow insignificant. But that smallness is less frightening than it is inspiring. It creates the reaction that Abraham Joshua Heschel frequently called "awe," a sense of marvel at the world's mystery and power. Somehow, our smallness and relative insignificance serve not to undermine our spiritual searching but to enhance it; awe creates the sense of being in the presence of something larger than we, a presence more majestic, eternal, and significant, a Power beyond us. Judaism's focus on *mitzvah*, the Tosafot suggest, is designed to create that same feeling in us on a daily basis.

Christian tradition understands this spiritual need well. The enormous European Catholic cathedrals like those in Chartres and Amiens provided many of the feelings people might have found in nature's majesty. But the genius of these cathedrals is that they created that response in the middle of the landlocked European continent, in the course of ordinary people's everyday lives.

While these cathedrals are more than seven hundred years old, their power lies not in their age, or even their beauty, as much as in their sheer size. People inside are dwarfed by the mass of stone that laborers fit together centuries ago. And not unlike the vastness of the ocean or the immensity of a glacier, the scale of the cathedral makes the worshiper feel tiny, insignificant, and, ironically, wholly at peace.

Upon visiting these cathedrals, Jews often implicitly ask themselves, "We don't have buildings like this. What does our tradition do to help us share this feeling?" What does Judaism do to evoke for us the feeling of God's enormity? How does Judaism capture the profoundly spiritual feeling of humility that these cathedrals evoke so successfully?

Strange though it may seem, instead of building cathedrals, Judaism focuses on *mitzvah*. How does *mitzvah* evoke for Jews the feelings that cathedrals create for Christians? It does so because *mitzvah* implies more than spiritual discipline and regularized behavior; it also implies an element of humility, of sensing ourselves as small in the context of God and of the enormity of the cosmos. *Mitzvah* captures some of the humility generated by both nature and cathedrals because central to the Jewish notion of commandedness is an emphasis on giving up control. By commanding behavior, *mitzvah* engenders an element of submission in Jewish life. That acquiescence to some other "authority," in turn, helps communicate the sense that we human beings are not the pinnacle of the cosmos. There is something in the world even more majestic than we are.

The idea of submission as part of religious or spiritual life does not come easily to us. Modern Western democracies, and therefore our most fundamental sensibilities, are almost all founded upon the principle that society must respect the individual and the individual's autonomy above almost everything else. Philosophers like John Locke (1632–1704), Jean-Jacques Rousseau (1712–1778), and John Stuart Mill (1806–1873), three of the giants who profoundly shaped modern liberalism, each argued in their own way that government was designed to serve the needs and rights of the individual. The state exists, many liberal theorists have argued, because individuals willfully decided to give up some of their autonomy—control over their destiny—in order to create an entity that could contribute to everyone's welfare and safety.

Today, centuries later, society still focuses on autonomy and the right of individuals to determine their future. This perspective spans the entire political and moral spectrum. On the political "right," the gun lobby asserts a Constitutional *right* to bear arms, while on the "left" the pro-choice movement insists that a woman has a *right* to control *her* own body. Ours is a culture that was founded on and now focuses on us: what we want, what we think we need, and how we want to get it.

By acting as a corrective to that one-sided perspective, *mitzvah* offers a crucial insight into Jewish spirituality. Nothing about Judaism denies the importance of the individual. Surely, the Torah's claim (Genesis 1:27) that all people are created in God's image suggests that Judaism takes the individual seriously. Chapter Seven will show that the Jewish system of ethics makes the same claim. But *mitzvah*, the system of Jewish commandments and obligations, seeks to remind Jews that in addition to rights, there are responsibilities. While human beings are significant, we are not all-important. Judaism and the system of *mitzvah* insists that there is something beyond us. We are not the ultimate standard. There is spiritual power in saying, as Jews do when the Torah is removed from the ark on Shabbat and they recite a prayer known as *Berikh Shemei* ("Blessed Is God's Name"), "I am a servant of the Holy One Blessed be He, before Whom and before Whose glorious Torah I prostrate myself." Spirituality is to be found, Jewish tradition suggests, not only in discipline, but in the notion of submission as well, for it is in the humility of submission that we sense something larger and more grand than ourselves in the universe. *Mitzvah* actualizes that idea.

THE THIRD FUNCTION OF *MITZVAH*: COMMANDMENT AS KEY TO JEWISH NATIONAL IDENTITY

Even beyond "spiritual discipline" and "humility/submission," however, *mitzvah* has other crucial roles to play. When Jews ask "Why be Jewish?" one important component of any answer has to be that in joining Jewish life, Jews participate not only in a religious or spiritual culture but in a national one as well. To be a Jew is also to be part of a people, a group that spans not only generations but continents, working in its own unique way to pursue its vision for the world. *Mitzvah* is a crucial element in Judaism's ability to make that claim. The next two functions of *mitzvah* that this chapter explores focus on *mitzvah* as key to Judaism's sense of uniqueness and the role of *mitzvah* in forging a distinct national Jewish identity.

The culture in which most modern Jews live is Christianity. When they seek to define the uniqueness of Jewish life, today's Jews often do so against a backdrop of Christian values and assumptions. One of the reasons that *mitzvah* is a crucial concept in describing Judaism's unique approach to spirituality is that it is in the realm of *mitzvah* that the profound differences between Judaism and Christianity become most clear.

Let's consider the writings of Paul, the man who essentially fashioned early Christian theology. As Paul (or Saint Paul as he is known to Christians) defined his emerging faith as distinct from Judaism, he felt compelled to repudiate the idea of *mitzvah*. In the Book of Romans, as he sought to describe exactly how people could live in an ideal fashion and achieve "salvation," Paul explained that after the death of Jesus (also a Jew), something dramatic had changed in the way people should achieve holiness and seek a relationship with God:

now we are rid of the Law, freed by [Jesus'] death from our imprisonment, free to serve in the new spiritual way and not the old way of a written law. . . . What I mean is that I would not have known what sin was had it not been for the law. If the [Torah] had not said [in the Ten Commandments] "You shall not covet," I would not have known what it means to covet. . . . when there is no law, sin is dead.

(ROMANS 7:6–8)

Notice how different this is from the Torah's viewpoint! The Torah suggests that observance of the commandments (or law, as Paul calls it) will lead to holiness; Paul believes, however, that law actually causes sin! This disparaging attitude to the law is reflected in numerous examples in many books of the Christian Bible; I'll refer to only two others, both of which are very well known.

Later in Romans, Paul discusses circumcision. In a dramatic departure from Judaism's worldview, Paul insists that what really matters is not whether a man is physically circumcised, but whether he reflects in his life the attitudes that circumcision addresses. Therefore, says Paul:

The real Jew is the one who is inwardly a Jew, and the real circumcision is in the heart—something not of the [law] but of the spirit. A Jew like that may not be praised by man, but he will be praised by God.

(ROMANS 2:29)

And in the Gospel of Matthew, Jesus makes a similar claim about keeping kosher (eating in accordance with traditional Jewish dietary regulations), insisting once again that it is not so much the actual law that matters, but the idea behind the law that is truly important. In what are now famous words, the Book of Matthew (15:11) claims that Jesus said, "What goes into the mouth does not make a man unclean; it is what comes out of the mouth that makes him unclean."

Ironically, early Christian tradition seems to have understood something that many Jews today fail to appreciate—*mitzvah* is part of the core of Jewish life. To live a religious life without command, without *mitzvah*, is to destroy one of Judaism's most important claims to uniqueness.

This insight, parenthetically, helps explain why both Jews and many Christians take offense at groups like Jews for Jesus. Judaism and Christianity each have their own unique paths to spiritual fulfillment, but they are very different. When it comes to *mitzvah*, a central feature of Judaism, Judaism and Christianity make virtually opposite claims. From a Jewish point of view, to claim that one can be part of both traditions is an affront to Jewish uniqueness and authenticity.

Christianity, no less than Judaism, strives to create a better world. Other religious traditions, no less than Judaism, encourage their believers to heighten their ethical sensitivities. What makes Judaism unique is its focus on *mitzvah* as a cornerstone of its spiritual path. Without Judaism's unique system of commandedness, it is often difficult to answer the question "Why be Jewish?" because Judaism seems so similar to other religious traditions. Without *mitzvah*, Judaism is robbed not only of one of its most profound sources of spirituality, but of its uniqueness as well.

THE FOURTH FUNCTION OF MITZVAH: JEWISH PEOPLEHOOD AND A SACRED MISSION

Finally, the importance of *mitzvah* culminates in its taking the notion of "uniqueness" and transforming Jews into a people. Peoplehood, a sense of sharing not only a religion, but language, culture, values, and history, has always been central to Jewish life. Indeed, it is that sense of sharing a national identity with other Jews that still animates many modern Jews' Jewish lives. But what we often fail to appreciate is that much of this sense of shared enterprise has traditionally been fostered by the notion of *mitzvah*. How? *Mitzvah* helps create transcendence not only by linking Jews to God, but by tying them to one another. Ironically, as we will see, the Jewish sense of peoplehood is closely tied to Judaism's sense of commandedness. Ultimately, to lose the latter is to profoundly weaken the former.

Most Jews, regardless of how committed or uncommitted they may be to Jewish life, sense their kinship with other Jews throughout the world. Jews often read the newspaper with a particular sensitivity to stories about Jews and Israel. Even Jews largely divorced from Jewish life find it difficult to vote for political candidates openly hostile to Israel. The plights of Soviet and Ethiopian Jews attracted the attention and concern of many committed Jews as well as those whose Jewish connections were more tenuous.

Why? Where does that kinship come from? Why did religious Jews in New York begin to lobby on behalf of mostly nonreligious Soviet Jews long before Soviet Jewry became a popular cause? What did they have in common? They did not share a language or even religious beliefs. They were practically as different from each other as people could be, but those American Jews lobbied, marched, and protested until their government began to act. Why? What was the bond they felt?

Why did Israeli pilots risk their lives to fly clumsy passenger jets into Ethiopia in the middle of a civil war suspended only by a tentative cease-fire to bring to Israel a band of Jews of a different race, language, tradition, and culture, who had virtually no formal education? Who were these people that those pilots should risk their lives for them?

They were Jews. Jews have the sense that they are one people, part of one shared enterprise.

This sense of partnership with other Jews involves more

than mere ethnicity, and goes beyond an instinctive impulse to band together for the sake of self-preservation. What is the source of that link? Why does the Talmud's claim that *kol yisrael arevim zeh ba-zeh*, "all Jews are responsible for one another" (Shavuot 39a), seem to have taken root?

These are some of the truly unanswerable questions of Jewish life. No one can fully explain the connection that Jews often feel to one another. For a long time, Jews did not ponder this connectedness too intently. Jews were so excluded from the prevailing culture around them that it seemed inevitable that they would form a closely knit, mutually supportive community. But as secular society has begun to welcome Jews, and even as many Jews have left many of their overt ties to Jewish life behind, this sense of kinship and mutuality remains. No explanation suffices. But Jewish tradition has always attributed part of the explanation to *mitzvah*. For *mitzvah* implies something not only about Jews and their relationship to God, but about Jews and their relationship to one another.

This distinct role for *mitzvah* is suggested in one of God's most often quoted instructions to the Israelites on their way from Egypt to the Promised Land. Shortly before Moses receives the Ten Commandments, the Torah reports that:

> Moses went up to God, and the Lord called to him from the mountain saying: This is what you shall say to the house of Jacob, and tell to the children of Israel. "You have seen what I did to the Egyptians, and how I carried you on the wings of eagles and brought you to Me. And now, if you listen to My voice and keep My covenant, you will be for Me a treasured people. . . . And you will be for Me a kingdom of priests and a holy nation."
>
> (EXODUS 19:3–6)

In the very same sentence, God stresses both the importance of command—"if you listen to My voice and keep My covenant"—and the concept of Jewish peoplehood—"you will be for Me a treasured people . . . and a holy nation."

In part, the commandment to become a "kingdom of priests and a holy nation" suggests the centrality of morality in Jewish life, a step to spirituality which I will discuss in Chapter Seven. But *am kadosh*, the notion of Jews as a holy nation, is about more than morality. It is about even more than the covenant between the Jews and God, a covenant expressed by *mitzvah*; it is about a unique relationship that makes Jews a people. Ultimately, *mitzvah* is about more than vertical connectedness; its focus is horizontal, too. The centrality of command and the importance of obligation in Jewish life do more than connect Jews to God; these ideas connect Jews to one another, creating of Judaism not only a religion but a people as well. How does *mitzvah* function this way?

Mitzvah, the Jewish link to covenant, conveys the sense that all Jews are partners in a shared and sacred enterprise. *Mitzvah* is one of the ways Jews express their belief that their purpose in living is to make the world a better place for their having been here through uniquely Jewish means. To be a Jew is to be part of a covenantal community of human beings, bound together in pursuit of a sacred and common purpose. To be a Jew, the concept of *mitzvah* implies, is to have inviolable responsibilities, not only to God and to the world, but to other Jews wherever they may be and, indeed, to the entire world. "The Jewish people, Torah, and God are all one," claims the Zohar, Judaism's most important mystical text. *Mitzvah* makes the same claim. Jews know that the sense of obligation that they feel to live in a certain way and to realize certain visions for the world is not an individual one. They know that other people share that sense of obligation. And almost without realizing, they feel a sense of connectedness, even kinship, with those other persons. They discover themselves as part of a people.

The idea of commandedness is part of the foundation of what Jews call *ahavat yisrael*, the love of one's fellow Jews. *Aha-*

vat yisrael does not imply loving Jews by ignoring non-Jews, nor does it suggest that all Jews agree about important issues. It certainly does not even mean loving or even liking all Jews in the way we love and like other people in our daily lives. *Ahavat yisrael*, an ancient and crucial Jewish concept, implies that Jews owe one another the respect and devotion that comes from being partners in a sacred cause. *Ahavat yisrael*—and the system of *mitzvah* that lies at its core—expresses our conviction that, ultimately, there is a deep and largely inexplicable feeling of connectedness that Jews feel with one another, a sense that, by being part of the Jewish people, they are part of something timeless, glorious, and of cosmic importance. The Jewish responsibility to be "a kingdom of priests and a holy nation" is no less a part of what brings spirituality to Jewish life than anything else discussed thus far.

When Jews decide that they want a *bris* for their sons, they often do not have the vocabulary to articulate what they want from the *bris*. But what they would say, if they knew how, is that being a Jew involves more than identifying with an ethnic group. It is more than choosing a religion. It is participating in an enterprise of connecting ourselves to something larger than us. Part of the transcendence that Jewish life provides comes from connection to God. But part of it also comes from connection to the Jewish people, and *mitzvah* conveys that as well.

MITZVAH: A DIFFICULT CONCEPT FOR MODERN JEWS

Because a worldview based on *mitzvah* is in many ways so vastly different from what most modern Jews are used to, many people wondering about how to begin a spiritual odyssey understandably ask: "Aren't there many committed and involved Jews who live rich and meaningful Jewish lives without *mitzvah* at their core?"

Yes. There *are* many committed Jews who live Jewish lives without *mitzvah* as a central feature of their Jewish lives. There are also Jews for whom God is not an issue, and Jews who feel no intimate connection to Jewish texts; there are, in fact, Jews in whose Jewish lives spirituality plays no role at all. The issue isn't whether or not such constructions of Jewish life are legitimate; the important point is that for those Jews who do want a substantive spiritual dimension to their Jewish lives, wrestling with God, encountering ultimate questions through Jewish sacred texts, and seeking transcendence through Jewish ritual are all important building blocks along the way. The same is true of commandedness, of "the details" of the system called Jewish law, or *mitzvah*.

For many modern Jews, another question about *mitzvah* arises almost immediately. Does *mitzvah* mean that Judaism is about absolute submission? Does serious Jewish life imply that I no longer make decisions for myself? Does Judaism really advocate a mechanical obedience in all areas of life and at all times?

While reading philosophers like Yeshayahu Leibowitz might suggest that Judaism is that mechanical and restrictive, important thrusts of Jewish tradition suggest otherwise. The famous story of the Oven of Achnai is a case in point. The Talmud tells that Rabbi Eliezer and the other sages disagreed about whether a certain oven was permissible for use, and neither side could convince the other. Then, the Talmud relates:

> On that day R. Eliezer brought forward every imaginable argument, but they did not accept them. Said he to them: "If the law agrees with me, let this carob tree prove it!" Thereupon the carob tree moved a hundred cubits from its place. . . . "No proof can be brought from a carob tree," they retorted. Again he said to them: "If the law agrees

with me, let the stream of water prove it!" Whereupon the stream of water flowed backward. "No proof can be brought from a stream of water," they rejoined. Again he urged: "If the law agrees with me, let the walls of the schoolhouse prove it," whereupon the walls inclined to fall. But R. Joshua rebuked [the walls], saying: "When scholars are engaged in a legal dispute, you have no right to interfere." Therefore, they did not fall, in honor of R. Joshua, nor did they resume the upright, in honor of R. Eliezer; and they are still standing thus inclined.

Again he said to them: "If the law agrees with me, let it be proved from Heaven!" Whereupon a Heavenly Voice cried out: "Why are you disputing with R. Eliezer, seeing that in all matters the law agrees with him!" But R. Joshua arose and exclaimed: "It is not in Heaven." What did he mean by this? Said R. Jeremiah: "The Torah had already been given at Mount Sinai; we pay no attention to a Heavenly Voice, because You wrote long ago in the Torah at Mount Sinai, 'After the majority must one incline.' "

R. Nathan met Elijah and asked him: "What did the Holy One, Blessed be He, do in that hour?" "He laughed [with joy]," he replied, "saying, 'My children have defeated Me, My children have defeated Me.' "

(Bava Meẓia 59b)

Not all of Jewish tradition sees the submission implicit in *mitzvah* as absolute. Here, the Talmud says that when the rabbis ignored God's heavenly voice and insisted on their right to decide the legal matter themselves, God laughed with glee and said, "My children have defeated Me."

God's acquiescence to this apparent *chutzpah* is all the more astounding when we realize that when Rabbi Jeremiah quoted the Torah as saying "after the majority must one incline" (Exodus 23:2), he had consciously misquoted! What the Torah actually says is "after the majority one must not incline," but Rabbi Jeremiah chose to omit the first Hebrew word, *lo* (meaning "no") from his quote, changing the entire intent of the verse. And yet, God raises no objections. The Talmud suggests that God relishes human input in the legal process; if submission is one end of the spectrum, Jewish tradition also recognizes and validates the other, which we might call human activism.

The tension between submission and activism is the struggle that animates much of modern Jewish denominational life. How far can Jews go in shaping the tradition to the needs of modernity and of current ethical insights before we lose the sense of submitting to something higher than ourselves, before we re-create Judaism in our own image? When does submission become so overwhelming that it threatens to suffocate the human dignity implicit in Judaism's tradition of intellectual sparring and inquisitiveness? These questions defy easy answers or formulations; ultimately, the richness of Jewish life is lived in the struggle between humility and activism, between the ideals of human discovery and human submission.

Much of the richness of Jewish spiritual exploration and living comes from the lifelong process of working to find a personal place on this spectrum that speaks to us, that reflects both elements of the tradition in a way that moves us spiritually and challenges us intellectually, too. Much of the richness of American Jewish life stems from the fact that different communities have found varying ways of accomplishing this goal. Those American Jews who already take *mitzvah* seriously have constructed a variety of theologies as foundations for their commandedness. They disagree about whether the commandments were revealed, when, and how. They pray in different ways, and from different books. They disagree about the ideal roles for women in Jewish life and on many other vital topics. That unending debate is where the genius of American Jewish pluralism shines; nothing about a return to *mitzvah* mandates an end to that creativity.

Of course, getting to a place in our own lives where we actually feel commanded by *mitzvah* is not always easy. For Jews who accept the standard theological argument that God has commanded the *mitzvot* and that their authority is therefore absolute, feeling commanded is somewhat easier. But even there, it is not automatic, and there are many Jews who accept God's authorship of the Torah and still struggle to work the discipline of *mitzvah* into their lives.

For other Jews, less certain about the origins of the Torah and God's role in creating the commandments, the path can be even more difficult. But let's not forget that the primary arguments for *mitzvah* in this chapter were not theological; they had to do with how *mitzvah* communicates the power, coherence, and uniqueness of Jewish life. Growing to a point of working commandedness into our sense of ourselves as Jews requires not necessarily theological reasoning, but help in internalizing what are here only abstract concepts. That depends largely on two additional factors: spiritual mentoring and life in community. We will turn to those parts of the Jewish spiritual journey in Chapter Eight.

What matters for now, as we embark on our odyssey, is not how we choose to express *mitzvah*, but that we choose it as one of the starting points. What matters now is not that we commit to every possible Jewish commandment, but that we start with some as we struggle to find a place for *mitzvah* in our personal odyssey. For what we now know is that Judaism's emphasis on command is not outmoded or irrelevant. It is the key to the ties that Jews make—to God, to one another, and ultimately to transcendence. That alone demands that we think deeply about the place of *mitzvah* in the Jewish lives we are building.

◇

Does God really care about the details? Perhaps that is the wrong question at this point in our journey. Perhaps the more important question is "Can we get from Jewish life what *we* want without the details?"

Probably not. Rabbi Ḥaninah understood this when he claimed that "Greater is the one who is commanded to perform a deed and does so, than one who is not commanded to perform that deed but does it." Giving charity, serving the community, helping the oppressed—all of these are immensely worthy actions. But when they are also *mitzvot*—expressions of commandedness—they become even more compelling. When rituals (and the ethical practices that I will discuss in Chapter Seven) become part of a system of *mitzvah*, they bind us in relationships of commitment, to God and to other Jews throughout the world. In that way, they link us to Judaism's profound spiritual depth.

Jews don't build cathedrals; we don't have Notre Dame to put us in touch with God, our spiritual selves, and our people. For us, *mitzvot* create that sanctity and convey that power. That is why *mitzvah* is key to Judaism's search for transcendence, why it is a crucial step on the Jewish quest for spirituality. It is one of Judaism's greatest challenges, but one of its richest rewards as well.

CHAPTER SIX

◆

PRAYER — JEWISH SPIRITUALITY AND THE STRUGGLE TO BECOME

◆

IRONICALLY, THE COMPONENT OF JEWISH SPIRITUALITY that I have left almost for last is often the first one that Jews encounter. It is the world of Jewish prayer. Jewish prayer makes use of many of the elements of spirituality that we have already discussed: words are central to the liturgy; prayer is highly ritualized; and it is one of Jewish life's most important *mitzvot*, commandments. Yet prayer is possibly also one of the most difficult elements of the Jewish path to spirituality; that is why we come to it only now. What is Jewish prayer about? How does it work? Wherein lies its spirituality?

For many Jews, nothing could seem less spiritual than the world of traditional Jewish prayer. It seems to reflect the very opposite of struggle. Our traditions tell us when to pray, whether to stand or to sit, what words to say, and, at times, even what to think about when we pray. With all of that, how can one feel part of a religious search, a spiritual odyssey? Where in that controlled experience do we struggle with our most profound and personal commitments?

It seems that of all the elements of Jewish life, prayer should be the most spiritual—and yet it disappoints us. We do not necessarily expect that observing Jewish law will always feel fulfilling, nor do we imagine that contemplating the abstract theological issues raised in Jewish texts will necessarily always move us. Yet when we enter a synagogue, we expect to be transported; we often desperately hope that the experience will not only comfort us but will leave us profoundly touched. Yet for many people, that rarely happens. Especially with prayer, we experience a tremendous gap between our expectations and reality.

That disappointment is partially unavoidable. Most of us can recall experiences in which we tried to recapture some particularly moving moment, yet found that reliving the ritual did not enable us to rekindle the emotions we wanted to feel. We returned to a restaurant where we once felt passionately in love with someone, hoping that a visit to the *place* would allow us to experience the *feeling*. We listened to a favorite song or piece of music, hoping to recapture the sentiments we once felt but now miss. But we also know that such "rituals" do not always have the impact we seek.

Thus, we ought to begin by recognizing that prayer isn't intrinsically powerless or empty just because it doesn't always provide the emotional intensity that we would like. Nothing in human life elicits an emotional reaction with complete regularity. Still, we do expect some satisfaction from prayer, and many Jews rarely feel it. Indeed, many Jews sense that in prayer they confront not the most spiritual element of Jewish life, but one of the most stultifying and frustrating.

In the pages that follow, we'll look closely at some of these issues. The discussion will first address some general ideas about Jewish prayer, and will then focus on some specific examples of Jewish prayer, most notably the *Amidah*. Throughout, we will seek to discover those areas in which the world of traditional Jewish prayer has the capacity to be not overwhelming or disappointing, but energizing and, in fact, deeply spiritual.

OUR AGENDAS FOR PRAYER

Prayer is difficult, even in the best of circumstances. But part of the problem may lie in the expectations we bring to it; often, our assumptions about the role of prayer virtually condemn our experience to failure. Let's look briefly at three of our common assumptions about prayer so we can gradually learn to transcend them and create the possibility of more meaningful encounters with the Jewish liturgical tradition.

PRAYER AS SEEKING COMFORT

Most of us expect prayer to inspire and comfort us. The grandeur of the synagogue, its architectural beauty and music, the peacefulness of the setting—all of these convey the sense that Jewish prayer is about feeling peace. We expect that participating in a service will touch us uniquely and deeply. So when we do not feel that peace, we feel let down.

But if Jewish life is about struggle, we should be suspicious of the assumption that prayer is entirely about peace or comfort. If prayer were designed only to provide comfort, would it contribute to our struggle? Probably not. If prayer were designed only to move and to touch us, if comfort and joy were its only goals, Jewish prayer would actually undermine the difficult effort involved in Jewish spirituality.

That is why Jewish prayer tries to evoke not only peace and comfort, but wrestling and angst as well. Despite our desire to feel beauty and the comfort that often accompanies it, it may be precisely when we feel somewhat disconcerted and not entirely at ease that Jewish prayer may be accomplishing its most central goal. Indeed, that ideal for prayer is communicated by the very word that Jews use for the act of praying.

The Hebrew term for the verb "to pray" is *le-hitpalel*, which means "to judge oneself," or even "to struggle with oneself." When we begin to examine a few examples of classic Jewish prayer later in this chapter, we will see that serious self-examination—hardly a perpetual source of comfort—figures centrally in some of Judaism's most central liturgies.

Jewish tradition urges us to pray not for comfort, but for growth. The Yiddish word for synagogue, *shul*, sounds like the German word for "school." In Jewish terms, both schools and synagogues are places of learning, of growth, and often of hard work. The best relationships are built, the tradition suggests, by intensive and ongoing effort. Judaism suggests that our "relationship" with our spiritual selves is no different. We relish comfort when we feel it, but ultimately, comfort is not what the Jewish liturgy is designed to provide. As a reflection of our ongoing struggle with our faith and with ourselves, Jewish prayer cannot always be comforting; occasionally, it must even be exhausting.

PRAYER AS A "WISH LIST"

Perhaps as a result of our earliest education about prayer, many of us approach prayer with a second misconception; we believe that prayer is essentially a "wish list," an inventory of things we would like God to provide for us. Most people, at some point in their lives, have turned toward heaven to express deeply personal and profound wishes. Sometimes we consciously conceive of this act as prayer; at other times, we may be shocked to find ourselves believing that any such request could do any good. Either way, we often sense that prayer is about asking for things.

But what about Judaism's openness to skepticism? If we do not believe that there is a God who hears our prayers, what could the purpose of prayer be? Similarly, if God hears us but cannot or will not answer our prayer, why should we bother? When we do pray for something we desperately want and we do not receive it, we feel betrayed. Particularly when what we want is someone's health or even the most basic financial security and we do not get that, our frustration with prayer often leads to our feeling abandoned by God. When that happens, ironically we feel worse after praying than we did before.

As we continue our exploration of prayer, we will need to examine carefully to what extent Jewish prayer is actually about petition at all. Of the three traditional components of Jewish prayer—praise of God, petitions, and giving thanks—which represents the most prominent portion? And when certain sections of some prayers do make requests, what is the nature of those requests? Can we always judge easily whether or not they have been answered? Does the liturgy believe there is value to making the request even if it is not answered? Might that, too, be part of the struggle? We will turn to these questions shortly.

PRAYER AS "CATECHISM"

Finally, many of us bristle at encounters with the traditional *siddur*, or prayer book, because we imagine that our tradition would have us feel entirely comfortable with every concept expressed in its pages. When we come across passages in the prayer book that we find difficult to accept, we feel unauthentic, inadequate, hypocritical. At these moments, the *siddur* suddenly seems an outdated catechism that does not deserve our serious attention.

This conflict raises other important questions. If our tradition believes that words are important, why does *it* tell *us* what to say? Does the tradition not understand that each of us is a different spiritual personality, and that no two of us make identical faith-claims? Should we say the things in the prayer book that disturb us, or does intellectual honesty demand that we omit them?

SPONTANEITY VERSUS FIXEDNESS

The tension between what the *siddur* says and what we actually believe is a crucial issue for modern Jews, and it leads our discussion to one of the most central tensions that the rabbis themselves felt about prayer. Even the sages of the rabbinic period, many of whom were responsible for the creation of much of our liturgy, were aware of this tension. Although the results of their work seem extraordinarily fixed and even impenetrable, they, too, recognized the tension between expressing our most passionate hopes and fears and reciting a set formulaic prayer. Consider this passage from the Mishnah, which discusses which version of the prayer known as the *Eighteen Benedictions* (also known as the *Amidah*, or *Silent Devotion*) an individual should recite:

> Rabban Gamaliel says, One must recite the *Eighteen Benedictions* every day. Rabbi Joshua says, One need only recite an abbreviated form of the *Eighteen Benedictions*. Rabbi Akiba says, Those who can read the prayers fluently should recite the full *Eighteen Benedictions*, but those who cannot [read fluently] should recite the abbreviated form.
>
> (MISHNAH BERAKHOT 4:3)

In this passage, the sages clearly express their sense that formulaic prayer is essential. The tradition refers to this sort of prayer as *keva*, which means "fixed." The Mishnah above is committed to the notion of *keva*. The only argument the rabbis seem to have is which version of the *keva* certain people must recite.

But the picture that emerges from the tradition quickly becomes more complicated. In the very next sentence, another sage offers a very different perspective:

> Rabbi Eliezer says, When someone makes their prayer *keva*, their prayer is not prayer.
>
> (MISHNAH BERAKHOT 4:4)

Rabbi Eliezer, one of the great rabbinic sages of the late first century, seems to be denying not only the importance but even the value of *keva*. Instead, he seems to insist on what the tradition calls *kavvanah*. The word *kavvanah* means many things, among them "intention"; but in the context of prayer, it refers to the spontaneous expressions of our innermost feelings, rather than the fixed, formulaic conception of prayer.

Since the days of Rabbi Eliezer, Jewish tradition has done a great deal to incorporate the value of *kavvanah* into the liturgy. Not only are Jews permitted to utter their own prayers as part of a service or at other times, the traditional prayer book even provides special opportunities to bring personal prayers into the very rubric of the formal liturgy. During the *Amidah*—perhaps the most central part of the liturgy (and a prayer I will discuss at length)—the *siddur* includes a special passage in the plea for health in which each individual is encouraged to add the names of people he or she knows who are ill.

Traditional Jewish prayer further personalizes worship by enabling each person to almost surreptitiously insert her or his name into the service. Jewish tradition claims that every person has his or her "own" biblical verse. This verse corresponds to the person's Hebrew name and either contains that person's name or, more often, begins with the first letter of the Hebrew name and ends with the last letter of the Hebrew name. Thus, for example, the verse for a person named Yizḥak (the Hebrew for Isaac) is Psalms 107:14, because the first letter of that verse is a *yod*, which is the first letter of the name Yizḥak, and the last letter of the verse is a *kuf*, which is the final letter of that name.

Many traditional Jews add their verse to the very conclusion of the *Amidah*, reciting it immediately prior to the last two sentences of the final paragraph. This custom is a way of personalizing prayer, of creating a reminder that the thoughts and passions in prayer must be our own, despite the fact that many of the words we recite were written by others. It deeply reflects Rabbi Eliezer's conviction that prayer has to be personalized to have meaning.

But as much as Rabbi Eliezer insists on *kavvanah*—intention—and argues that *keva*—fixed prayer—is an insufficient form of prayer, we must not misconstrue his position. As a sage of great importance, he was clearly not denying that Jews were obligated to recite the *Eighteen Benedictions*. He, too, undoubtedly recited them daily. What Rabbi Eliezer wanted to remind us, however, is that there is a perennial tension between the formulaic and the spontaneous in Jewish prayer.

Jewish tradition has never denied the importance of *keva*. The fixed times of prayer are necessary, our tradition has argued, precisely because we struggle with faith. Our struggles, because they are so real, demand the constancy that *keva* provides us.

Jewish tradition provides not only a fixed schedule for prayer but a fixed formula as well. The formula of the liturgy is necessary, Jewish tradition holds, as it affords us a place to begin our prayer. How do we address a Being we cannot see or know? What do we say to a God we are not always certain is there? For many of us, the challenge is so great that we would be unable to start. The *keva* of the Jewish prayer book is there to assist us when we cannot find our own words. Ultimately, we may hit our stride and find something to say. But just as the opening lines of a deeply personal letter can be the most difficult to write, so, too, the beginning words of prayer can be the most elusive. That is what *keva* provides for us. It provides the way to start when our own self-consciousness or lack of imagination might otherwise get in the way.

Keva, the formulaic nature of Jewish prayer, serves yet another important function: it creates community. We've seen that creating community is an important part of other elements of Jewish life such as the study of text, ritual, and *mitzvah*; prayer is no exception. As different individuals—each with her or his own hopes, fears, and doubts—come together to recite the same words, a community is born. Were we each to recite our own thoughts in our own way and at our individually chosen times, we would rarely pray together. But since we do recite the same words, and because we need each other for a *minyan*, or traditional prayer quorum, we find ourselves praying with other people. And as we see that they, too, struggle with faith and with belief, we are reminded that we can also join the chorus of seekers, even though our hearts and intellects sometimes rebel. For many of us, this feeling is most palpable when we recite the mourner's *Kaddish*. At moments of loss, our desire to be part of a community overcomes the barriers that often keep us away from synagogues at other points in our lives.

There is a power in communal recitation and singing that an individual's experience cannot elicit. That is why the tradition insists on *keva*. Without *keva*, we would never experience the energy of communal prayer. But with only *keva*, the tradition insists, we lose a sense of our own spiritual searching. Somehow, difficult though it may be, Judaism insists that we try to retain both.

How do we accomplish that? Is it really possible to recite the formulaic prayers that make up the liturgy and still express our personal thoughts and feelings at the same time? As we saw, Jewish tradition accomplishes both of these goals by urging us to compose our own prayers and insert them throughout the service. But while this is an important element of prayer, it is not sufficient. For if we express our own spiritual search in prayer only when we add our own materials, what is the point of the rest? If *keva* and *kavvanah* are mutually exclusive, why the *keva*? Must we resign ourselves to a cold and mechanical experience when reciting the fixed liturgy? Perhaps even the fixed liturgy is much more open to our personal searches than we might have imagined. Let's consider one popular example.

ADON OLAM: EXPRESSING THE STRUGGLE EVEN IN THE FORMULA

Once we begin looking carefully at the poetry of the *siddur*, we begin to note that *keva* and *kavvanah* are not as mutually exclusive as we might originally have believed. Even in the midst of the *keva*, the tradition urges us to challenge, to wonder, to grow. Even in the formulaic, the prayer book urges spontaneity and the expression of our most personal struggles and quests.

Let's return to the question of God, and our suggestion that Judaism recognizes how difficult it can be to sustain faith. Does the difficulty of that struggle find expression anywhere in the *siddur*?

One of the most well known poems in the entire prayer book is *Adon Olam*. Though the poem has been attributed to Solomon ibn Gabirol of the eleventh century, its origins are actually unknown. Nonetheless, it is commonly recited, not only at the conclusion of the Sabbath service, but at the beginning of the morning service and immediately before going to sleep at night. In some communities, it is also recited by those who are present at a deathbed.

What does this poem say about God? Its ten lines read as follows:

> *The Lord of the world was king before any creature was*
> *   formed;*
> *At the time when all came into being by His will, His*
> *   name was proclaimed King.*
> *And even after all things shall have come to an end, He*
> *   alone, awesome, will remain King.*
> *And He was, and He is, and He will be in Glory.*
> *And He is one, and there is no second to compare with*
> *   Him, to place beside Him.*
> *Without beginning, without end, and His is the power and*
> *   the dominion.*
> *And He is my God, my living redeemer, a Rock in my tra-*
> *   vail at the time of distress.*
> *He is my Banner and my Refuge, the portion of my cup*
> *   when I call.*
> *To His hand I entrust my spirit, when I sleep and when I*
> *   wake.*
> *And with my spirit, my body also. God is with me; I shall*
> *   not be afraid.*

On the surface, this poem seems to bespeak absolute faith in God. It focuses on God's absolute power and timelessness, seemingly unconcerned with the struggles that many of us have with these sorts of postulates. But if that is the case, how did the poem become so popular? Has the poet nothing more to say? Is this nothing more than a rote recitation of God's awesome qualities?

When we look closely, we see that there are really two sections to this poem, with the split coming after the sixth line. In the first six lines, the poet summarizes some common claims about God: God has always existed, God still exists, and there-fore, presumably, God will always exist. Similarly, God is without compare, majestic unlike any other being in the world.

But suddenly, after line six, the tone changes. Beginning with the seventh line, the focus shifts. The poet moves away from broad theological claims about God's grandeur, focusing instead on the speaker's intimate feelings about God. No longer is God endless and majestic; now, the poet speaks of "*my* God . . . a Rock in *my* travail at the time of distress." Gone are the claims that "even after all things have come to an end, God alone, awesome, will remain King"; in their stead we hear "to His hand I entrust my spirit, when I sleep and when I wake." Just as the Mishnah we examined above abruptly switched its emphasis from *keva* to *kavvanah* from one line to the next, this text suddenly focuses not on what we believe about God, but on how we feel about God.

Note which of these two emphases the poet chooses as the closing of the poem. Is the author perhaps suggesting—however subtly—that ultimately what matters in Jewish life are not our abstract concepts of God but our struggle to feel God's presence? Is this prayer echoing the attitude to God that we first encountered in Chapter Two? Is it possible that *Adon Olam* specifically speaks of our feeling God's presence when we go to sleep, because it is when we sleep that we lose control of our thoughts, our appearance, and even our body? Perhaps this prayer wants to say, "Ultimately, we all struggle with God. But at certain moments of spiritual intimacy, it does not matter what you believe about God. That is not why we pray." Why do we pray? Because for each of us, there are moments of darkness, of fear and of deep loneliness, when we desperately want to sense the presence of the cosmic. At those moments, we invoke not the God of the theologians, but the Presence who is our refuge, our redeemer, our companion. *Adon Olam* urges us not to think, but to feel; to quest not for certainty but for closeness. If we can sense that closeness and its warmth, the *siddur* reminds us, we are spiritually well on our way.

Notice how different is this sense of *Adon Olam* from that

with which we began. At first blush, this prayer seemed to demand that we proclaim concrete beliefs. It reminded us of "prayer as catechism," invalidating our struggle and denying the legitimacy of our questions about God. But the *siddur*, like all sophisticated poetry, demands careful reading and openness. When we shed the hostility we often bring to traditional prayer, we find something very different from what we expected. We discover validation of our search, a reconfiguration of the very goals of prayer. We encounter prayer not as obstacle but as advocate, and we discover a new, validated role for the liturgy in our spiritual odyssey.

Adon Olam is hardly the only example of this dimension of Jewish prayer. Many other elements of the prayer book validate this sort of searching. Some even lead us along the quest, gently navigating our path on the way. Even prayers that we call "petitional," prayers that make requests of God, ultimately seek not to request but to navigate our spiritual journey. The weekday *Amidah* is a classic case in point, to which we now turn.

THE DAILY *AMIDAH*: THE HIDDEN SPIRITUALITY OF SIMPLE REQUESTS

Earlier in this chapter, I suggested that another obstacle to our finding meaning in traditional Jewish prayer is the series of "requests" that periodically appear in the prayer book. Many of us find these requests—commonly called "petitions"—difficult either because we do not believe they will be answered, or because we desperately need them to be answered, and we all too often feel they are ignored. Either way, why should we say them?

In order to answer this difficult question, let us now turn our attention to the *Amidah*. The *Amidah* is a complicated prayer, and our question is a difficult one. Thus, this next section is a little more lengthy than others, but a discussion of this sort is necessary if we are to take our appreciation of prayer further.

The *Amidah*, also known as the *Eighteen Benedictions*, is the central prayer of the Jewish liturgy. Indeed, many classical rabbinic sources refer to it as *ha-tefillah*, or "the prayer." Not only is the *Amidah* the central prayer of the Jewish liturgy, but in its most common formulation, most of it consists of relatively specific requests of God. Therefore, for many modern Jews, the *Amidah* rekindles those very questions about prayer as a "shopping list." Let's turn now to a brief look at the *Amidah*, to ask whether these paragraphs are, in fact, a simple "shopping list," or whether even the penitential portion of Jewish prayer might also lead to spiritual searching.

On the surface, the *Amidah*'s text is not complex. At first glance, it is simply a series of paragraphs, each of which ends with a blessing. The central section of the weekday *Amidah*— perhaps the tradition's most pivotal prayer—begins as follows:*

You graciously endow mortals with intelligence, teaching us wisdom and understanding. Grant us knowledge, discernment, and wisdom. Praised are you, Lord, who graciously grants intelligence.

Bring us back, our Father, to Your Torah. Our King, draw us near to Your service. Lead us back to You truly repentant. Praised are You, Lord, who welcomes repentance.

Forgive us, our Father, for we have sinned; pardon us, our King, for we have transgressed, for You forgive and pardon. Praised are You, gracious and forgiving Lord.

Behold our affliction and deliver us. Redeem us soon because of Your mercy, for You are the mighty Redeemer. Praised are You, Lord, Redeemer of the people Israel.

---

*This interpretation of the *Amidah* is deeply influenced by Professor Reuven Kimmelman (Brandeis University) and his unique readings of Jewish liturgy.

Heal us, O Lord, and we shall be healed. Help us and save us, for You are our glory. Grant perfect healing for all our afflictions. For You are the faithful and merciful God of healing. Praised are You, Lord, Healer of the people Israel.

Lord our God, make this a blessed year. May its varied produce bring us happiness. Grant blessing upon the earth, satisfy us with its abundance, and bless our year as the best of years. Praised are You, Lord, who blesses the years.

Sound the great *shofar* to herald our freedom, raise high the banner to gather all exiles. Gather the dispersed from the ends of the earth. Praised are You, Lord, who gathers our dispersed.

. . .

Grant true and lasting peace to Your people Israel and to all who dwell on earth, for You are the supreme Sovereign of peace. May it please You to bless Your people Israel in every season and at all times with Your gift of peace. Praised are You, Lord, who blesses the people Israel with peace.

Is that it? Is there nothing more that the most central Jewish prayer has to say? Would we not expect something more significant from the *Amidah*? And how could we ever suggest that such a simple text might serve as a subtle guide for our spiritual odyssey? Let's look at these paragraphs somewhat more closely. Why do we find them in this particular order?

A Plea for Knowledge and Understanding

What would we imagine would be the first request that the *Amidah's* penitential section would make? A request for our own health? Someone else's health? Financial security? Liberation from the personal struggles that torment us?

Very few of us would likely name a request for "knowledge,

discernment, and wisdom" as the first thing for which we would ask when addressing God. Why, then, does the *Amidah* give that plea such important standing? Why not start with the requests that first come to mind? The reason is that the *Amidah*—even in its penitential section—addresses not our common desires for the tangible things in life, but our craving for a meaningful spiritual life. While this section does begin with "requests," they are not the requests we might expect. Jewish tradition recognizes that often the deepest human desires ultimately point in one clear direction: our realizing how little of the world we truly comprehend and our profound need to understand more.

The *Amidah* begins by reminding us of our desperate desire to understand our world; it also recalls for us our everlasting inability to comprehend all that we would like to. But we can never give up our perennial struggle to understand more, so the prayer book exhorts God, "Grant us knowledge, discernment, and wisdom. Praised are You, Lord, who graciously grants intelligence."

TORAH AS THE SOURCE OF KNOWLEDGE

Immediately, however, the *Amidah* suggests to us that our search for knowledge and understanding is not entirely hopeless. When overwhelmed by the incomprehensibility of the universe, Jews have traditionally turned to Torah and our other sacred texts (all of which we call Torah) for precisely this kind of understanding. Whether the story of the Binding of Isaac or Moses' discovery that absolute truth is not accessible to us—or any other selection, for that matter—our texts are the places to which we have turned for spiritual growth and moral depth, the sources we employ to begin our analysis of life's imponderables. Thus, as soon as the *Amidah* reminds us how much more we would like to understand, it essentially tells us how to go about that. It states, perhaps more to us than to God, "Bring us back, Our Father, to Your Torah."

But authentic encounters with Torah are not simple ones.

When we discover ourselves in Torah, we also discover our faults. We recognize the myriad of ethical or ritual expectations we do not meet. When we confront examples of bravery, we have to face those instances in which *we* did not have the courage to stand up for what we knew was right. As Jewish texts remind us of the power of language, we cannot ignore our tendencies to abuse language, to let hateful speech go unchastised. When we study Torah, we often discover what is noble about humanity; yet we also uncover what is less than noble in our own lives. Suddenly, our search for knowledge has led us to a sense not only of the limited nature of our understanding, but of our moral and spiritual flaws as well. Therefore, immediately after the *Amidah* reads "Bring us back, Our Father, to Your Torah," it continues, "Lead us back to You truly repentant. Praised are You, Lord who welcomes repentance." The subsequent paragraph focuses even more directly on our perceptions of our own inadequacies as it beseeches God, "Forgive us, our Father, for we have sinned; pardon us, our King, for we have transgressed, for You forgive and pardon. Praised are You, gracious and forgiving Lord."

DISCOVERING THE HUMAN NEED FOR REDEMPTION

Rather unexpectedly, what had seemed to begin as simple request has now turned the focus to us, to our failings, to our continued need for growth. And as our simple requests have now turned to an admission of the many ways in which we need to improve, we suddenly realize how difficult it will be to make many of those changes.

True change is something that we achieve only with tremendous difficulty. It is often much easier to *say* "I'm sorry" than to *be* truly sorry. Real repentance, Jewish tradition claims, requires a *lev nishbar ve-nidcheh*—"a shattered and contrite heart" (Psalms 51:19). But it is not easy for anyone to become so utterly displeased with who they are. Most people will go to great lengths to avoid such feelings. We find it easier to apologize than to be utterly shattered and to vow in our heart of hearts that we will not repeat an action again. The Psalmist claimed that God was the "healer of shattered hearts" (Psalms 147:3), and many of us want exactly that kind of comfort from our religious tradition. But sometimes encounters with God shatter the heart. We realize not only how imperfect we are, but how difficult it will be to change.

That is why the *Amidah* then continues, "Behold our affliction and deliver us. Redeem us soon because of Your mercy, for You are the mighty Redeemer." Essentially, the prayer book now begs God to help us fight the most important battles of our lives. We recognize that there are things that we do that we do not wish to do, but we also know that we are sometimes too weak to avoid them. So we turn to God, broken and shattered, and say, "We need You to help redeem us, for we cannot redeem ourselves alone."

At times, however, we become so devastated, so thoroughly unhappy with ourselves, and so overwhelmed by the difficulty of changing ourselves that we begin to believe there is virtually no hope. When we are so weak, we ask ourselves, how dare we expect redemption from anywhere, even from God?

Perhaps that is why the next paragraphs of the *Amidah* plead with God to "heal us, O Lord, and we shall be healed," and then continue: "Lord our God, make this a blessed year. May its varied produce bring us happiness. Grant blessing upon the earth, satisfy us with its abundance, and bless our year as the best of years." Maybe the liturgy accounts for the sense that we all grow doubtful of God's redemption; maybe the *siddur* knows how often we have felt disappointed. Therefore, the *Amidah* follows the prayer for redemption with two concrete examples of ways in which we have been redeemed. If we have ever been in the slightest bit ill—and all of us have—we know that we have somehow gotten better. That in itself, the prayer book suggests, is a small miracle, a redemption. We know how lonely it is to be sick; we rebel against the weakness, the loss of energy, and the lack of control over our bodies that even the most minor illness brings. Yet when we recover, we often take our healing for granted, failing to appreciate the miracle that a properly functioning body is.

Is Personal Redemption a Possibility?

When we most doubt the possibility of redemption, the liturgy would have us recall that each of us has received his or her own personal redemption, even in those seemingly innocuous moments in which we are healed from some illness. And we have also experienced the power of God's redemption, the liturgy adds, as communities. When the *Amidah* continues to beseech God for a year of plenty, the liturgy reminds us that there is redemption in places where people do not go hungry, when threatening rains and storms abate, and when drought is followed by rainfall. It makes no difference whether we believe that God actually caused these redemptions or whether they stem from some other source; on at least one level, all the *Amidah* wants is for us to reexperience those moments of healing and of hope, and to gain from those memories the courage to continue our struggle for growth and insight.

The prayer book reminds us of these small but significant moments of redemption in our lives. It believes that we will find the courage and strength to continue to work for our own redemption, and we will continue on the spiritual quest that is so central to Jewish life. And the *Amidah* expresses its conviction that we will find such courage as it moves toward ever greater dreams and hopes. First, the liturgy expresses the hope that the Jewish people will be redeemed. In classical Jewish terms, that prayer for a healed people finds expression in the image of a God who will "gather the dispersed from the ends of the earth." Once the *Amidah* has succeeded in convincing us of the possibility of the repair and renewal of Jewish existence, it gradually moves to the prayer of which we are all too quick to despair. The final petition of the *Amidah* implores God, "Grant true and lasting peace to Your people Israel and to all who dwell on earth, for You are the supreme Sovereign of peace."

Perhaps now we can begin to rethink our previous assumptions about the petitional dimension of Jewish prayer. As we discussed, many of us approach the traditional liturgy and its occasional requests of God with a feeling that verges on hostility. Why should we utter these requests when we are not convinced that God hears us? What is the value of these supplications when we all know that heartfelt and genuine prayers sometimes go unanswered?

The traditional liturgy, the "petitional" function of prayer, is more complicated than it may initially seem. Our brief glance at the *Amidah* suggests that, more than anything else, these petitions are designed first to help us recognize our failings and to remind ourselves how desperately we wish to grow and to learn. Once we have come to that realization, the liturgy tries to encourage us to remain open to the possibility of redemptions in our own life—from whatever source we may believe they come—and to persevere in our commitments to improve ourselves and our world. If we can accomplish that, the tradition believes, our prayers on their most profound level have, in fact, been answered.

PRAYER AS A FORUM FOR PERSONAL STRUGGLE

This discussion of the *Amidah* offers us a useful opportunity to return to our common concern that prayer all too often seems catechism-like, listing for us things that the *liturgy* seems to think we ought to believe, rather than reflecting *our own* concerns and struggles.

Yet one other dimension of the *Amidah* virtually demands

our attention, for perhaps more than any other element of the
Jewish liturgy, it reminds us that Jewish prayer is ultimately not
concerned with reciting what someone else thought we *should*
believe, but with growing and searching, with discovering
what each of us *can* believe.

The opening phrase of the *Amidah* is well known because it
appears in every Jewish service. It reads: "Praised are You, Lord
our God and God of our ancestors, the God of Abraham, the
God of Isaac, and the God of Jacob." Some traditional commentators have asked why the text reads "the God of Abraham, the God of Isaac, and the God of Jacob" rather than "the
God of Abraham, Isaac, and Jacob." Why the repetition of the
phrase "the God of"? What does that duplication add? It reminds us, several commentators have suggested, that Abraham, Isaac, and Jacob did not all have the same conception of
God. The repetition of the phrase comes to reiterate our fundamental claim that because Abraham, Isaac, and Jacob were
all distinct human beings, their thoughts and beliefs about
God simply had to differ. And if Abraham, Isaac, and Jacob all
had conflicting and varying conceptions of God, surely *we*,
who live in a very different place and time, must be permitted
that freedom.

But the phrase "the God of Abraham, the God of Isaac, and
the God of Jacob" has implications that go even further than
the notion that all of us inevitably think about God in our own
unique and personal ways. For in the entire Bible, God is re-
ferred to as "the God of Abraham, the God of Isaac, and the
God of Jacob" only twice. And both of those instances are in
the third chapter of the Book of Exodus, which was discussed
in Chapter Two.

What is the context of that chapter? It is the story of the
burning bush. Let's review it briefly. As Moses senses God's
presence in a bush that is caught in fire but is not consumed,
God commands Moses to go to Egypt and to demand that
Pharaoh free the Israelites. Moses, overwhelmed and fright-

ened, responds that he does not wish to go. So he responds to God and asks, "When I come to the Israelites and say to them 'The God of your fathers has sent me to you,' and they ask me, 'what is His name?' what shall I say to them?" It is then that the phrase that we now recognize from the *Amidah* comes into play. As the Torah continues, we read:

> And God said to Moses, "*Ehyeh asher ehyeh.*" [God] continued, "Thus shall you say to the Israelites: '*Ehyeh* sent me to you.'" And God further said to Moses, "Thus shall you speak to the Israelites: 'The Lord, the God of your ancestors, the God of Abraham, the God of Isaac, and the God of Jacob, has sent me to you. This shall be My name forever, This My appellation for all eternity.'"

In the mind of the traditional Jew, the phrase "the God of Abraham, the God of Isaac, and the God of Jacob" is thus inseparable from the phrase "*Ehyeh asher ehyeh,*" or "I will be what I will be." Thus, each time the traditional liturgy opens the *Amidah* with the phrase "the God of Abraham, the God of Isaac, and the God of Jacob," it reminds us that when Moses demanded to know God's name, all God could say was "I will be what I will be." God's essence, or at least our perception of it, is always in the process of forming, perpetually developing. And in light of that, prayer cannot expect us to believe anything so particular.

As we learned earlier, Moses was ultimately frustrated in his search for absolute truth. Initially propelled by a desire to understand God, he came to learn that such comprehension is beyond the capacity of human beings. Prayer, then, is about recapturing the sense of wonder forced upon Moses. We open the *Amidah*—and traditional Jews do so three times each day—and encounter a phrase that is specifically designed to suggest that God's essence is becoming, and that if we are created in God's image, then we, too, must be perpetually becoming. For us, Jewish life is ultimately about growing, searching, and yearning—taking part in a lifelong spiritual odyssey.

Jewish prayer is not catechism. Judaism is too respectful of our individuality, our minds, and our personal struggle to demand that prayer become a recitation of a series of "I believe" statements. Nor is Jewish prayer about asking for a variety of tangible goods or outcomes. And finally, the Jewish liturgical experience is not even designed to make us feel good or comfortable at every moment.

Though we have examined only a few examples of Jewish prayer, we have seen enough to realize that our initial assumptions about Jewish prayer were not entirely on target. Jewish prayer, like Jewish life, is about spiritual growth. It is about wonder, about awe. It recognizes our fear, and our fear of fearing. It demands work, but not absolute or unthinking submission. It respects and validates our struggle, and claims that as we confront ourselves—what we are proud of and what we most desperately wish to change—we do the most important work in human life.

It was Yeats who said that when we argue with others, we create rhetoric, but when we argue with ourselves, we create poetry. That poetry of self-examination is the stuff of which our liturgy is made. The *siddur* seeks not to constrain, but to enable. Prayer, though very difficult, is but a reflection of the search that is Jewish life. It demands our attention and our seriousness, but it does not demand that we give up being who we are. Ultimately, prayer—like all Jewish life—validates much of who we are, and insists that with effort and with some fortune we can become even more thoughtful and more caring human beings, inching ever closer to the expression of God's image that is at the very foundation of each and every one of us.

◇

CHAPTER SEVEN

JEWISH ETHICS

AS A

PATH TO

TRANSCENDENCE

◇

YESHAYAHU LEIBOWITZ, THE MODERN ISRAELI PHI-losopher encountered in Chapter Five, makes an interesting claim about Jewish tradition. He writes that Judaism is:

> a religion of the ordinary, unexceptional individual who is not necessarily blessed with a spiritual disposition. . . . [Judaism] is not enthusiastic about the ecstatic, unusual episodes of one's spiritual life, the "holiday" moments of

life, so transient and momentary. . . . Judaism renders religion the prose of life.[*]

Leibowitz puts the point somewhat too strongly. As we have seen, it is not true that Judaism is uninterested in ecstatic feelings or "holiday" moments. Much of Jewish life, in fact, is designed precisely to create those moments. Yet Leibowitz is absolutely on target with regard to Judaism's celebration of the mundane. He is correct when he suggests that much of Jewish tradition is about the prose, not the poetry, of life. What Judaism offers Jews is a tradition that not only colors and enriches periodic ecstatic and celebratory moments, but that also tries to transform daily, ordinary life into a religious, spiritual encounter.

How does Judaism do this? In part, Jewish tradition makes use of the regular study of sacred texts, a dietary code, blessings, prayer, and other rituals to sanctify the ordinary. But Jewish life takes seriously yet another avenue on the path to spirituality—the everyday interactions between people, the realm of human life we commonly call ethics. Jewish tradition makes the claim that God can be sought, and even experienced, as we build relationships with other human beings. Judaism takes seriously the Torah's claim that each and every human being is created in God's image (Genesis 1:27); it claims that when each human interaction is seen as an interaction with the Divine, with a person created in God's image, ordinary human life begins to acquire a more profoundly spiritual dimension.

---

[*]Yeshayahu Leibowitz, "Commandments," ed. Arthur Cohen and Paul Mendes-Flohr, *Contemporary Jewish Religious Thought* (New York: The Free Press, 1987), p. 68.

THE CENTRALITY OF ETHICS
IN JEWISH LIFE

Many people tend to see the worlds of the spiritual and the mundane as intrinsically conflictual; they see ritual and ethics as distinct and unrelated. The first, they suggest, is a matter of our quest for transcendence, our search for spiritual fulfillment, while the second ensures that the "nonspiritual" world in which we live is safe, habitable, and cordial. Although Judaism has distinct terms for rituals (which it calls *mitzvot bein adam la-makom*, or commandments between God and people) and ethics (which it names *mitzvot bein adam la-ḥaveiro*, or commandments between people), it denies a radical separation between these two categories. Jewish tradition insists that everyday life, and particularly the realm of morality in ordinary human interactions, has a profound capacity to enrich our spiritual existences. The words we use, the charity we give, the ways we invite people into our homes, and even how we make love are all part of Jewish life's broad path to spiritual encounter.

The first hints of this linkage appear as early as the Torah itself, most particularly in the Book of Leviticus' *Parashat Kedoshim*, or Holiness Code. A slightly abbreviated version of this lengthy passage reads as follows:

The Lord spoke to Moses, saying: Speak to the whole Israelite community and say to them: You shall be holy, for I, the Lord your God, am holy. You shall each revere his mother and his father, and keep My sabbaths: I the Lord am your God. Do not turn to idols or make molten gods for yourselves: I the Lord am Your God.

When you sacrifice an offering of well-being to the Lord . . . it shall be eaten on the day you sacrifice it, or on the day following; but what is left by the third day must be consumed in fire. . . .

When you reap the harvest of your land, you shall not

reap all the way to the edges of your field, or gather the gleanings of your harvest. You shall not pick your vineyard bare, or gather the fallen fruit of your vineyard; you shall leave them for the poor and the stranger: I the Lord am your God.

You shall not steal; you shall not deal deceitfully or falsely with one another. You shall not swear falsely by My name, profaning the name of your God: I am the Lord.

You shall not defraud your neighbor. You shall not commit robbery. The wages of a laborer shall not remain with you until morning. You shall not insult the deaf, or place a stumbling block before the blind. You shall fear your God: I am the Lord. . . .

You shall not hate your kinsman in your heart. Reprove your neighbor, but incur no guilt because of him. You shall not take vengeance or bear a grudge against your kinsfolk. Love your neighbor as yourself: I am the Lord. . . .

You shall not let your cattle mate with a different kind; you shall not sow your field with two kinds of seed; you shall not put on cloth from a mixture of two kinds of material. . . .

When you enter the land and plant any tree for food, you shall regard its fruit as forbidden. Three years it shall be forbidden for you, not to be eaten. In the fourth year all its fruit shall be set aside for jubilation before the Lord; and only in the fifth year may you use its fruit—that its yield to you may be increased: I the Lord am your God.

You shall not eat anything with its blood. You shall not practice divination or soothsaying. You shall not round off the side-growth on your head, or destroy the side-growth of your beard. You shall not make gashes in your flesh for the dead, or incise any marks on yourselves: I am the Lord. . . .

You shall rise before the aged and show deference to the old; you shall fear your God: I am the Lord. When a stranger resides with you in your land, you shall not wrong him. The stranger who resides with you shall be to you as one of your citizens; you shall love him as yourself, for you were strangers in the land of Egypt: I the Lord am your God. . . .

I the Lord am your God who freed you from the land of Egypt. You shall faithfully observe all My laws and all My rules: I am the Lord.

(LEVITICUS 19:1–37)

There is much more in this seemingly simple passage than initially meets the eye. First of all, *Parashat Kedoshim*, the Levitical Holiness Code, gives a rationale for all of Jewish religious life; it begins with a statement that because God is holy, we, too, should be holy. Religious life, it suggests, is about trying to imitate God. It is not the essence of Judaism (the view of Yeshayahu Leibowitz discussed in Chapter Five notwithstanding) to live life in accord with God's command simply because God has commanded. The Torah suggests that *mitzvot*, or Jewish behaviors, are actually a means to an end. They are designed to create holiness. Jewish life is about creating holiness by providing guidelines for imitating God; in the words of the Midrash, "The commandments were given only for the purpose of purifying God's creatures" (Genesis Rabbah 44:1). Jewish life, ultimately, is designed to make us better people.

The second important element of the Holiness Code is that the Torah sees behavior as the crucial element of the path to holiness. Given what we now know about Judaism, it should come as no surprise that the Torah's prescriptions for achieving holiness are built on a foundation of daily behaviors. Throughout this book, we have seen that Judaism allows, and even fosters, a tremendous degree of intellectual latitude; Judaism's communal cohesiveness (what Emile Durkheim called "collective conscience") emerges from its communal behaviors, not from constraints on belief. Therefore, the Holiness Code does not suggest contemplation or solitary meditation as the path to holiness; it suggests that daily human activity is what enables us to become most God-like, or holy.

The third important element of Leviticus 19 emerges when we note the specific activities and behaviors that the Torah mandates. The very first behavior that the Torah lists as it lays out a path to holiness is "you shall each revere his mother and his father"; interestingly, the Holiness Code opens with a command about interpersonal ethics, not ritual. As the passage continues, the Torah offers countless other examples of interpersonal behaviors that it sees as keys to holiness. The Torah commands that we leave produce at the edges of the field so that the poor can collect the grain and sustain themselves. It prohibits theft, instructs the Israelites to refrain from gossip and slander, and reminds them to treat the stranger with compassion. And the list goes on. The Torah insists that daily human interactions are key to striving for *kedushah*, or holiness.

Finally, the fourth observation emerges not from the content of Leviticus 19, but from its organization. As one reads the passage, it becomes clear that ritual commands and ethical instructions are not neatly separated one from the other. Leviticus 19 begins by commanding us to be holy, and then continues immediately, "You shall each revere his mother and his father, and keep my Sabbaths." In the very same verse, the first command seems to govern interpersonal relationships, while the second, which follows immediately thereafter, turns to the realm of ritual—Shabbat in this case. Throughout the chapter, ritual and ethics are commingled. Their interdependence is expressed perhaps most clearly in 19:8, which states: "Love your neighbor as yourself: I am the Lord."

The juxtaposition of "Love your neighbor as yourself" and "I am the Lord" is striking. And it is not coincidental. The entire structure of Leviticus 19 seeks to make an important point about Jewish life and Jewish spirituality in general: the boundary between the ritual and the ethical is far from clear. Each depends on the other. Ethics and ritual work hand in hand as they seek to add a profound quality of spirituality to everyday life. A Judaism that matters, that speaks to the most profound human spiritual and emotional quests, needs both.

INTERPERSONAL RELATIONSHIPS AS A PATH TO GOD

On the obvious level, ethics play a crucial role in Jewish life because Judaism, like many other religious and ethical traditions, seeks to create a better, more harmonious world. Toward that end, it seeks to make people more sensitive and more responsive to those around them. Were this all that Jewish tradition had to say about the importance of ethics, Judaism might have little to add to what other traditions say. But to this "mundane" notion of ethics, Jewish tradition adds another claim: ethical behavior is important not only because it leads to a more perfect world, but because it leads to God.

The notion that morality is a distinctly spiritual endeavor sounds more poetic than useful. Does Jewish life actually consider ethical behavior an important component of the Jewish search for spiritual fulfillment? It does. Let's return to the Holiness Code introduced in the previous section, and specifically, the prohibition on insulting the deaf.

Why is insulting the deaf offensive, when deaf people cannot hear the curse? Many commentators offer a rather functional interpretation. For example, Rashi (1040–1105), the most important commentator on the Torah, suggests that the Torah uses the example of a deaf person to teach something about hearing people as well; the Torah wants to suggest that if we must be careful about how we speak about a deaf person, then surely we must be even more careful about how we speak about those who can hear.

But other commentators take a more consciously spiritual approach to this peculiar command. They interpret the entire verse in light of its final clause, "You shall fear your God: I am the Lord." Thus, for example, the *Itturei Torah* ("Crowns of the Torah," a twentieth-century anthology and interpretation of classical commentaries) argues that "all commandments that govern people's actions are designed to perfect their actions. Those commandments that govern their innermost thoughts are designed to perfect their hearts."

What does the *Itturei Torah's* comment have to do with insulting a deaf person? The *Itturei Torah* is suggesting that the reason for the command has nothing to do with the impact of the curse on the deaf person; the command is concerned with the impact of the curse on the person who utters it. The prohibition on insulting the deaf, the commentary of the *Itturei Torah* suggests, is designed to perfect not our actions but our thoughts. It is designed not only to protect the reputation of the deaf person (in itself, an important function), but perhaps even more importantly, to shape the way we think, react, and feel. When it insists that we not insult the deaf, the Torah is suggesting that there is more at stake in human relationships than not causing harm to others. Jewish tradition insists that our behavior also creates fertile spiritual opportunities. The Torah's ethic goes beyond a simple utilitarian calculus. Judaism wants more from human behavior than the avoidance of pain or injury; the tradition wants the way we behave to have an impact on how we feel and how we perceive the world.

Why is Jewish tradition so concerned with shaping how we feel? Part of the reason, no doubt, is Judaism's goal of "purifying God's creatures." But an equally important reason, though less commonly recognized, is that Judaism believes that the sensitivity that results from careful ethical behavior has the capacity to enrich those parts of our personality that enable us to build relationships with the transcendent, to feel God's closeness. Judaism insists that our behavior with other people has the capacity to lead us to new spiritual heights. This role for ethics emerges quite clearly in the following well-known passage from the Talmud:

> R. Ḥama son of R. Ḥanina . . . said: What is the meaning of the verse: "You shall walk after the Lord your God" (Deuteronomy 13:5)? Is it possible for a human being to walk after the *Shechinah* [God's presence]; for has it not been said: "For the Lord Your God is a consuming fire" (Deuteronomy 4:24)? But [the meaning is] to walk after the attributes of the Holy One, blessed be He. As He clothes the naked, for it is written: "And the Lord God made for Adam and for his wife coats of skin, and clothed them" (Genesis 3:21), so you must also clothe the naked. The Holy One, blessed be He, visited the sick, for it is written: "And the Lord appeared to [Abraham] by the oaks of Mamre [after his circumcision]," so you must also visit the sick. The Holy One, blessed be He, comforted mourners, for it is written: "And it came to pass after the death of Abraham, that God blessed Isaac his son" (Genesis 25:11), so you must also comfort mourners. The Holy One, blessed be He, buried the dead, for it is written: "And He buried him in the valley" (Deuteronomy 34:6), so you must also bury the dead.
>
> (SOTAH 14A)

The simplicity of Rabbi Ḥama's question disguises its profundity. Rabbi Ḥama's real question is not about the verse "You shall walk after the Lord your God," but about holiness. If God is so elusive, he seems to ask, where do we search? If God is ultimately unknowable, where do we find something tangible to hold on to as we seek the transcendent, as we quest for the spiritual?

Jewish tradition's response is that people are an important component of our link to God. Rabbi Ḥama is making what might seem a radical suggestion. He claims that though we cannot know God, we can foster our own spiritual growth by acting in the ways that we imagine God would act. Judaism asserts that if when we visit the sick, we do so with the sense that this is what God would do, the mere act of visiting the sick takes on a distinct spiritual quality. If when we comfort mourners we do so mindful of Judaism's tradition that God, too, comforted Isaac when Abraham died, a purely social visit suddenly ties us to a tradition, to a people. At ideal moments, it even creates a sense of God's closeness.

Thus, ethics in Jewish life are not only about creating a more perfect world (an ideal that we saw reflected in the world of ritual as well, particularly in the celebration of Shabbat). Ethics are also a link to Judaism's spirituality.

The idea that spiritual life can be lived only in the context of ethical life is reflected in countless other dimensions of Jewish tradition. Because classical Jewish tradition does not expressly use the category "spirituality" in its vocabulary, we do not find explicit statements linking "ethics" to "spirituality." Nevertheless, a sensitive reading of many sources suggests that while traditional texts did not articulate this sense of a linkage between morality and spirituality in any explicit manner, the relationship was very much on the minds of the rabbis who composed these classic works.

ETHICS AS A PATH TO SPIRITUALITY: THE EVIDENCE FROM TRADITION

Judaism expresses its claim that a concern with ethics is an integral part of the Jewish spiritual journey in a variety of ways. Sometimes, this argument takes the form of a typical moralistic aphorism. One source argues, for example, that:

> Whoever has an opportunity to perform an act of *tzed-dakah* (charity or kindness) and does not perform it, or whoever has an opportunity to save another person and does not, causes himself to die.
>
> (TANNA DE-VEI ELIYAHU ZUTA 1)

It is unlikely that the rabbi who composed that adage meant to imply that such a person would literally die. Rather, his point seems to have been that ignoring the plights of other people erodes a person's humanity, causing his or her "spiritual death."

Another example of this linkage. The *Kizzur Shulhan Arukh*, an abridgment of Judaism's major law code, is not known for its poetic style. Indeed, a terse, almost turgid prose has long been one of its hallmarks. The volume lists law upon law, often without explanation, and certainly without any theological poetics. But in the midst of this rather dry work, when the *Kizzur* comes to the laws of charity, something other than law makes its way into the text. In the opening section on the laws of *tzeddakah* (although commonly construed as "charity," it actually means "righteousness"), Rabbi Solomon Ganzfried (1804–1886, the author of this work) includes a long section on the values inherent in Jewish charitable giving. At one point, he writes:

> a person should always keep in mind the depth of his desire when he pleads before the Holy One Blessed be He. With the same intensity that he wishes that the Holy One Blessed be He will heed his cry, he should heed the call of the poor.
>
> (KIZZUR SHULHAN ARUKH 34:1)

Ganzfried's point is subtle but crucial. Charity and prayers to God inform each other. Jews should reflect on the intensity of their own needs when they beseech God, and should recognize that the needs of the poor have the same intensity. A person's spiritual life has to inform his ethical behavior. Similarly, recognizing the profound needs that the poor have should awaken him to his own needs, which can in turn nurture and enrich his experiences of prayer. That is why, parenthetically, Jewish tradition requires even the person living exclusively off of charity to donate back some of the charity she or he has just received. On a purely functional level, this process is obviously inefficient. But the tradition insists that the poor have spiritual lives as well, and that they, too, need the sensitivity that the giving of *tzeddakah* can provide.

It is in the world of prayer and liturgy that Jewish texts make the link between ethical sensitivity and spiritual openness most clearly. Consider the final paragraph of the *Amidah*, the pinnacle of Jewish prayer discussed in Chapter Six. This passage is commonly called *Elohai Nezor*, the words with which it begins. It reads:

> My God, keep my tongue from evil and my lips from
> speaking deceitfully. To those who curse me, let my soul
> be silent, and let my soul be as humble as the dust to all.
> Open my heart to Your Torah, that my soul might pursue
> Your commandments.

Note the progression in this passage. The poet begins with a plea that he be given the strength not to speak ill of anyone. He then asks for the self-control he will need to ignore those who speak ill of him, hoping that he can find the humility necessary for disregarding the pain they might cause him. Finally, having figuratively reached that level of humility, he dares to ask for closeness to God, and beseeches God, "Open my heart to Your Torah." It is humility before human beings, the poet implies, that lays the groundwork for achieving the humility we need in order to build a relationship with God. Even our daily choice of words, the poet suggests, has not only ethical implications, but spiritual ramifications as well.

Other passages evoke the linkage between ethics and spirituality in still other ways. In one well-known passage, the rabbis claim that the Temple, the archetypal repository of Jewish spirituality in Jerusalem, was destroyed not because of ritual sinfulness, but because of simple human cruelty:

> The destruction of Jerusalem came through a Kamza and a Bar Kamza in this way. A certain man had a friend Kamza and an enemy Bar Kamza. He once made a party and said to his servant, Go and bring Kamza. The man went and [mistakenly] brought Bar Kamza. When the man [who gave the party] found him there he said: "See, you tell tales about me; what are you doing here? Get out." Said the other: "Since I am here, let me stay, and I will pay you for whatever I eat and drink."
>
> He said: "I won't." "Then let me give you half the cost of the party." "No," said the other. "Then let me pay for the whole party." He still said, "No," and he took him by the hand and put him out.
>
> [Bar Kamza said to himself]: Since the Rabbis were sitting there and did not stop him, this shows that they agreed with him. I will go and inform against them, to the [Roman] government. He went and said to the Emperor: "The Jews are rebelling against you." He said, "How can I tell?" He said to him: "Send them an offering and see whether they will offer it [on the altar]." So [the Emperor] sent with him a fine calf. While on the way, [Bar Kamza] made a blemish on its upper lip, or as some say on the white of its eye, in a place where we [Jews] count it a blemish but [the Romans] do not.
>
> The Rabbis were inclined to offer it in order not to offend the government. R. Zechariah b. Abkulas [disagreed and said] to them: "People will say that blemished animals are offered on the altar."
>
> (GITTIN 55B–56A)

According to the story, the animal was therefore not offered on the altar, which the Emperor took as a sign that the Jews were, indeed, rebelling against him. As a result, the tradition has it, he decided to destroy Jerusalem and the Temple. The unnecessary humiliation of Bar Kamza at the party, the rabbis therefore say, ultimately led to the destruction of the Temple. Ethical insensitivity destroyed the holiest place in Jewish tradition. Without ethics, the tradition asserts, ritual and spirituality cannot survive.

But perhaps the most haunting illustration of Judaism's sense that treatment of other human beings has the capacity to either nurture our sense of God's presence or destroy it is found in the conclusion of the story about the Oven of Achnai, discussed in Chapter Five. Let's review the story briefly.

Rabbi Eliezer and the sages disagree about the ritual status of a certain oven. Rabbi Eliezer believes that it is usable, while the sages disagree. When he finds himself unable to convince them using standard legal arguments, Rabbi Eliezer begins to invoke miracles: a tree uproots itself, a stream flows backward, and the walls of the academy begin to tilt. After the sages disregard all the miracles that Rabbi Eliezer invokes, a Heavenly Voice (the Voice of God) seeks to intercede, and supports Rabbi Eliezer. But the sages tell the Heavenly Voice that now that the Torah has been given, even God may not interfere. God is banished from a discussion of God's law!

According to the Talmud, not only was God not upset with them, God was delighted. As we saw in Chapter Five, the Talmud says that God was laughing and saying, "My children have defeated Me, My children have defeated Me." The intriguing story evokes a sense of intimacy, an element of trust that abides between God and the sages who interpret God's Torah. God has faith in them, and they in turn seem fully cognizant that, even in their independence, they are entrusted with the protection of God's sacred law. There is a sense of shared enterprise, a mutuality even though God is excluded from the discussion. But that notion of partnership, of spiritual security, unravels as the story continues:

> On that day all objects which R. Eliezer had declared clean were brought and burnt in fire. Then they took a vote and excommunicated him. They asked, "Who will go and inform him?" "I will go," answered R. Akiba, "lest an unsuitable person go and inform him, and thus destroy the entire world." What did R. Akiba do? He donned black garments and wrapped himself in black, and sat at a distance of four cubits away from him. "Akiba," said R. Eliezer to him, "what matter of such import happened today?" "Master," he replied, "it appears to me that your companions are separating themselves from you." Thereupon he, too, rent his garments, put off his shoes, removed [his seat], and sat on the earth, and tears streamed from his eyes.
>
> (BAVA MEZIA 59B)

Suddenly, the image of the rabbis "victorious" over God gives way to an image of pure human tragedy. This is the story of a life forever altered, a reputation destroyed, a human being in ruins. As the Talmud continues, it makes clear that while God could tolerate being "evicted" from a discussion of the very Torah God had revealed, God could not abide the cruelty with which Rabbi Eliezer was treated:

> The world was then smitten: a third of the olive crop, a third of the wheat, and a third of the barley crop. Some say, the dough in women's hands swelled up.

Another tradition, which follows immediately on the same Talmudic page (this page, incidentally, is reproduced in Chapter Three), goes even further. Not only has Rabbi Gamaliel's arrogance disturbed the natural order, his cruelty was so profound that he seems to deserve death:

A scholar taught: Great was the calamity that befell that day, for everything at which R. Eliezer cast his eyes was burned up. Rabban Gamaliel, too, was traveling in a ship, when a huge wave arose to drown him. "It appears to me," he reflected, "that this is due to none other than R. Eliezer b. Hyrcanus." He then arose and exclaimed, "Master of the Universe! You know full well that I have not acted for my honor, nor for the honor of my father's family, but for You, so that strife may not multiply in Israel!" At that the raging sea subsided.

At this point, it seems that Rabbi Gamaliel's plea has been accepted. When he assures God that his actions were not for his own sake, but for God's, the sea subsides, and it appears that all will end well. But all cannot end well, for Rabbi Eliezer's pain is permanent. As a result, the story needs one final chapter, which again follows immediately:

Ima Shalom was R. Eliezer's wife, and sister to R. Gamaliel. From the time of this incident onward she did not permit him to fall upon his face [in petition of God]. One day . . . she found him fallen on his face. "Arise," she cried out to him, "for you have killed my brother." At that moment, an announcement was made from the house of Rabban Gamaliel that he had died. "How did you know it," [R. Eliezer] asked her. "I have this tradition from my father's house: All gates are locked, excepting the gates of wounded feelings."

Ima Shalom, Rabbi Eliezer's wife and Rabbi Gamaliel's sister, understands the depth of her husband's pain. She intuits that if his pain reaches heaven, God will kill the person who caused him to suffer. But that person was her brother. So she forbids her husband from supplicating God, to no avail. And when Rabbi Eliezer's prayers do reach heaven, her brother dies, because, as she puts it, "All gates are locked, excepting the gates of wounded feelings."

As the story ends, the sense of harmony and equilibrium that had been established between people and God has been completely destroyed. The olive, wheat, and barley crops have suffered. Storms have raged on the open sea, reflecting God's rage over the sages' treatment of Rabbi Eliezer. Though Rabbi Gamaliel's entreaty convinces God to stop the storm, Rabbi Eliezer's wounded feelings ultimately rise to heaven, and Rabbi Gamaliel is punished with death for his role in his colleague's humiliation.

The power of the narrative is heightened when we recall that Rabbi Eliezer is not the story's hero. Precisely the opposite is the case. Though God punishes those who humiliate him, he actually began as a (well-intentioned) villain. As far as the rabbis are concerned, Rabbi Eliezer's desire to let God settle their legal debate threatens to destroy rabbinic Judaism. The rabbis had worked long and hard to develop a religious system in which human logic and argumentation would determine rulings on Jewish legal issues. Rabbi Eliezer's consciously seeking God's intervention threatened to restore a former way of Jewish life that they thought they had transcended. Even the miracles he invokes suggest the danger of his method. He causes trees to uproot themselves and streams to flow backward, both of which had the capacity to destroy the largely agricultural society in which he lived. More clear, however, is the symbolism of the walls of the house of study. When the walls tilt in response to his call for a miracle, the Talmud is suggesting that invoking God's intervention threatens to destroy the very house of study and, indeed, to kill the rabbis inside. The sages who responded with such anger at Rabbi Eliezer did not do so without cause.

And yet, the Talmud says that they went too far. Excommunicating him, casting him out from society in total disregard of his reputation, was simply too much. And most importantly, while God could abide being told to stay out of the legal debate, God could not abide the pain caused to a well-intentioned human being. Ironically, casting God out of the academy created a sense of intimacy between God and the sages; casting Rabbi Eliezer out destroyed that relationship, and invoked God's most profound punishment on the key figures and their society. "You may ignore my legal rulings," God seems to say, "but you may not trifle with human beings." The punishment is death, which in this story must be seen as symbolic of the spiritual death that occurs when God's presence is "banished" by the impact of human insensitivity and cruelty.

How does Judaism seek to make this ethical behavior a reality? Does Jewish tradition simply exhort human beings to be kind, or does Judaism have some unique approach to realizing this ideal? As we saw in Chapter Five, Judaism employs the concept of *mitzvah*, or commandment, to add texture to the Jewish world of ritual. It does the same with Jewish ethics.

LAW AND JUDAISM'S ROAD TO ETHICS

The mere idea that law could be a road to ethics sounds counterintuitive to many people. They would claim, in the spirit of the passage from Paul's Letter to the Romans cited in Chapter Five and the spirit of much of Western Christian tradition, that ethics are better born of a sense of love than of the institution of command.

Judaism disagrees. In part, Jewish tradition has grown suspicious of other motivations for ethics because of Jewish history. Jewish tradition knows that in the name of love and the saving of souls, people were burned alive in the Spanish Inquisition. In the alleged pursuit of racial harmony for Germany and Europe, Hitler conspired with the German people to build a diabolical murder machine unlike anything humankind had ever witnessed. Judaism is unimpressed with humanity's record in the pursuit of lofty goals.

On much more mundane levels, Jewish tradition believes that no matter how well intentioned we may be, human beings are extraordinarily skillful at justifying whatever actions they wish to take. It is not that Judaism is intrinsically suspicious of human beings, though the tradition does express a healthy amount of skepticism about our motivations. It is simply that Jewish tradition sought to be honest about who and what we are. Noble though we may strive to be, Jewish life has long recognized that selfishness is difficult to overcome, that humility is difficult to attain, and that even when many people recognize that what they are doing is wrong, they persist in doing it anyway. Judaism seeks to respond to this reality by incorporating ethics into its system of law, or *mitzvah*.

Jewish tradition believes that in so doing it accomplishes at least two important goals. First, the details of the various *mitzvot* give guidance in potentially ambiguous situations and minimize the degree to which our innate skills at self-justification can enable us to skirt our responsibilities. Second, Jewish tradition believes that by incorporating ethics into the world of *mitzvah*, it can "raise the stakes." By suggesting that, to employ theological language, God cares about how we speak no less than about what we eat, Judaism has sought to communicate the idea that piety and authentic Jewish spirituality are not accessible to those who disregard the tradition's ethical teachings.

Judaism's "legal" approach incorporates much more than the world of charity, which has already been briefly discussed. Rabbi Israel Meir Ha-Kohen (1838–1933, better known as the *Ḥafeẓ Hayyim*, the name of his most important work) wrote an entire book on the matter of speech: When is it permissible to share information about people, and when is it not? If someone is about to enter into a professional relationship with someone about whom we have unflattering information, may we share that information in order to steer the person away from the agreement? What actions must we take to make sure that we do not even hear someone else speaking ill of others?

Indeed, the laws, or *mitzvot*, of Jewish ethics extend to almost all walks of human interaction. They cover human sexuality, noting that a husband is obligated to provide for his wife's sexual satisfaction and specifying, depending upon his profession, how often he must do so (Ketubbot 62a). Jewish tradition gives specific instructions on how to visit the ill (*Kizzur Shulhan Arukh* 193:1–4). It says that the visitor must not sit on the sick person's bed, it specifies what times of the day are appropriate for visits, describes what to discuss with the ill person, and even mandates the way in which bad news should be shared with him or her.

Consider this further indication of the link between ethical behavior and Judaism's interest in spirituality: the law even notes that if a person visits a sick person but leaves without having been moved to pray on their behalf, he or she has not fulfilled the obligation to visit the ill. Simple human interactions and Jewish spirituality are intrinsically connected.

Judaism's *mitzvot* also govern treatment of animals (*Kizzur Shulhan Arukh* 191). The tradition notes that it is forbidden to cause an animal pain, and even notes that if a person passes a horse having trouble in pulling a cart, he is obligated to help the horse so that the horse's owner will not be tempted to beat the animal. The laws of Jewish ethics are also concerned with the use of words and gestures, even when they seem to cause no harm. Jewish law forbids the offering of a gift that a person knows will not be accepted (63:5), it prohibits asking about the price of an item if we have no intention of buying it (63:2), and forbids anyone from reminding a person who has repented of their previously sinful ways (63:2). Ultimately, Jewish tradition asserted that as important as it is to guarantee the kosher status of certain foods and the ongoing study of Torah, it is no less important to guarantee that basic interpersonal commandments can also be performed. It is not that one is more important than the other; both are essential for the sort of life that Jewish tradition seeks to make possible. The following Talmudic tradition about the cities in which scholars should live makes the point clearly:

> A scholar should not reside in a city where the following ten things are not found: A court of justice that imposes corporeal punishment and decrees penalties; a charity fund collected by two and distributed by three; a Synagogue; public baths; a restroom; a physician [for performing circumcision]; a surgeon; a notary; a slaughterer; and a schoolmaster.
>
> (SANHEDRIN 17B)

It is not sufficient, the Talmud suggests, to live in a community where there is a slaughterer to provide kosher food, a physician to perform circumcision, and a schoolmaster to teach children Torah. A habitable city must also have a system of justice and a charity fund. Indeed, the only function about which the Talmud specifies the number of people is the charity fund, not any of the ritual roles.

Whether this passage was intended to be applicable law or simple hyperbole is debatable but not important for our purposes. What emerges from this text and from the hundreds of other texts in the Jewish tradition that govern people's fulfillment of their responsibility for one another is that these social functions were seen as *religiously* significant. Lives of meaning, lives of spiritual questing, Jewish tradition asserts, require ethics no less than ritual and *mitzvah*.

And the system apparently worked. While modern Jews must be careful not to romanticize Jewish life in Eastern Europe, it was apparently nonetheless true that as poor as those Jewish communities often were, Jews did not starve. Almost all boys received the rudiments of an education (the education of girls was unfortunately considered less important at that time), orphans were cared for, widows were not cast off, and a sense of obligation for one another did prevail. Indeed, as the members of those communities gradually emigrated to the United States in the late 1800s and early 1900s, they created the benevolent and social organizations that became one of the hallmarks of early American Jewish life. Most of these people were not religious, and many were not particularly learned. But they came from a community in which the ethical and spiritual values of the tradition spoke even to those not interested in exploring them, because they were lived. Through the medium of law, *mitzvah*, obligation, Jewish communities translated these values from the "poetry" to the "prose" of life. As a result, even those people who never explored the poetry were touched by the fundamental values of what Jewish life stood for.

MITZVAH AND RITUAL AS KEY TO JUDAISM'S ETHICAL SOPHISTICATION

The link between Jewish ethics on the one hand and *mitzvah* and ritual on the other has had at least one other important implication. Through the sophistication of Jewish texts and ritual, Jewish tradition has enabled Jews to explore ethical issues that do not arise on a daily basis and that, because they are so theoretical, Jews might not think about at all. As a case in point, let's examine briefly the ritual known in Jewish life as Shabbat Zakhor.

In traditional Jewish life, the Shabbat before the holiday of Purim is called Shabbat Zakhor. Haman, the villain of the Purim story, is said to have been a descendant of the tribe of Amalek (I Samuel 15:8 and Esther 3:1). Because Purim celebrates the Jews' undoing of Haman's plot to destroy them, Jewish tradition mandates that on the Shabbat before the holiday, Jews read how they were attacked by Haman's ancestors, the tribe of Amalek. Indeed, tradition indicates that it is not enough to read the passage, but that every adult Jew is responsible for hearing each and every word of the reading. While normally the reading of the Torah is attended by seriousness but not overwhelming tension, at this moment in traditional synagogues, an absolute silence takes over, children are frequently reminded to be quiet, and an entire community strains to hear each and every word.

The passage that tradition selected for reading does more than review the historical record. It is about memory, with an important twist:

> Remember what Amalek did to you on your journey, after you left Egypt—how, unfettered by fear of God, he surprised you on the march, when you were famished and weary, and cut down all the stragglers in your rear. Therefore, when the Lord your God grants you safety from all your enemies around you, in the land that the Lord your God is giving you as a hereditary portion, you shall blot out the memory of Amalek from under heaven. Do not forget!
>
> (DEUTERONOMY 25:17–19)

The silence and tension of that moment in the synagogue, combined with the awesome responsibility conveyed in the Torah's command, force us to ask important questions. What are the things in life that are important to remember? Are we remembering enough? Are we passing it on? To our children? To theirs? To society?

Other questions emerge. How can we both "remember what Amalek did to you on the journey" and at the same time "blot out the memory of Amalek"? Does not the command to "blot out the memory" preclude the performance of the command to "remember"? Perhaps the Torah seeks to allude to more subtle, but complicated, questions. Is it important that the past be remembered? Are we better off destroying the memory of evil or preserving it? Why?

The more one examines the ritual of Shabbat Zakhor, the more it becomes clear that this particular *mitzvah* also raises profound ethical questions. Can the preservation of the past get in the way of forging a new future? Jewish tradition demands that Jews remember with indignation all that Amalek did to them. But at the same time, it also insists on a spirit of forgiveness and spiritual growth. In Exodus 23:9, the Torah warns, "You shall not oppress a stranger, for you know the feelings of the stranger, having been strangers in the land of Egypt." How ought Jews to balance the command to remember with the obligation to forgive? In the aftermath of the *Shoah*, how ought Jews honor the dying wishes of many of their fellow Jews who begged those who survived never to forget them, to remember to tell their story? Is it important also to make way for forgiveness? How will Jews and Judaism fairly perpetuate those memories (and the impressions they create of Germans) in only a few years, when all those who were alive in 1945 have died?

The ritual of Shabbat Zakhor and its texts claim that memory is a complicated tool with important ethical implications. But these are ethical issues that law cannot simply resolve through specific instructions. Nor are they issues that arise every day in our regular interactions with other people. Part of the wisdom of Jewish tradition, part of what it has to offer Jews who seek it, is its unique way of combining attention to ritual with a seriousness about ethical inquiry. Much of Judaism's uniqueness and richness stems from this combination of spiritual approaches.

DOES THE ETHICAL TRADITION "WORK"?

Does Judaism's approach to ethics imply that Jews are more ethical than non-Jews? Certainly not. Not only does Jewish tradition not deny the possibility of moral life outside Judaism, it even celebrates people it calls *hasidei umot ha-olam*, or "the righteous ones of the nations of the earth." Does Judaism's particular approach to morality, the building of ethics through *mitzvah*, guarantee that all Jews will act morally? Again, clearly not. Not only does Jewish tradition recognize that not all Jews will observe the laws, it even admits that a person can be a *naval bi-reshut ha-Torah*, a "disgraceful person within the boundaries of the law." Jewish tradition has never been naive about people or the ability of any ethical tradition to shape everyone. It understands that every religious tradition is marred by the occasional misdeeds of hypocrites, and that no religious community is immune to the persistent threat of fanaticism or fundamentalism.

Nonetheless, Jewish tradition insists that its distinctive approach to ethics has value. It would argue that given the realities of human nature, law is still an ideal way to encourage ethical behavior. Judaism argues that mandating the details of ethical behavior communicates a sense of urgency about ethics. Most importantly, Jewish tradition asserts that in linking ethics to spirituality, it affords Jews an important way to build a life of meaning, to create daily moments filled with spiritual significance.

All too often, modern Jews misjudge the role of ethics in Jewish life. They point to outwardly pious Jews who behave in obviously unethical ways, and suggest that Judaism stresses the ritual at the expense of the ethical. But that is clearly not true. Or they ask, "If one can be outwardly pious but still unethical, who needs Jewish ethics?" To which Judaism responds that Jewish ethics do shape the values of many people, and that for those who take Judaism's ethical system seriously, it provides not only ethical guidance but deep spiritual substance as well.

Alternatively, other Jews proclaim that Judaism's main contribution to the world has been its ethical system, and that modern Jews today can live a full and nurturing Jewish life by concentrating on Judaism's ethical system, without the "baggage" of ritual, *mitzvah*, Jewish texts, and the like. But that perspective is equally flawed. For what we have seen is that the depth and texture of Jewish ethics emerge from their unique linkage to those other parts of the Jewish spiritual journey. Without Jewish texts, rituals, and *mitzvah*, what makes those ethical behaviors uniquely Jewish? Aren't there many non-Jews who behave every bit as ethically as the most ethically minded Jew? Of course there are, and the best of Jewish tradition has never denied that.

Jewish ethics matter only in the context of a rich and textured Jewish life. In partnership with the other dimensions of Jewish life that we have examined, they offer not only a unique means of improving the world but a consistent, thoughtful, intellectually sophisticated, and spiritually satisfying means of adding depth, consequence, and meaning to the relationships that make up the world in which we live. That is precisely what many modern Jews want—even demand—from Jewish life, and that is what the combination of study, intellectual honesty, ritual, prayer, *mitzvah*, and ethics of Jewish life has to offer.

CHAPTER EIGHT

WHAT IS JUDAISM? WHERE TO BEGIN THE JOURNEY? WHY JUDAISM?

A POPULAR JEWISH QUIP CLAIMS THAT IF YOU ASK two Jews a question, you will get three answers. Most jokes have their serious side, and this one is no exception. It points to something this book has been highlighting since the very first chapter: Judaism is not a simple, neatly packaged system of belief. While Judaism speaks loudly and clearly on many moral and religious issues, it is also a tradition of struggle, of search, and of deliberation. For people seeking easy answers to difficult questions, Judaism might thus seem unsatisfying. But for people interested in exploring life, spirituality, and meaning to their fullest, Judaism has a unique, rich, and multivalent tradition to enrich both the questions and the process of searching for answers.

To be sure, Judaism is more than a tradition designed to imbue our lives with meaning. There are many important elements of Jewish tradition that this book has not addressed. Except in the most cursory of terms, I have not discussed Jewish history. One of the greatest miracles of modern Jewish life is the rebirth of the State of Israel, and I have also not discussed Israel or Zionism in any detail. Judaism has rich musical and artistic traditions, and they, too, have received insufficient attention in these pages.

No book can do justice to all of Jewish tradition. My purpose has been to focus on only one dimension of Jewish life, the part of Judaism that most directly addresses the spiritual yearnings that all human beings feel at various moments of their lives. That is not because spirituality is necessarily a more important dimension of Judaism than any other, but because it is spirituality that many modern Jews seek, and it is spirituality that they all too often claim they cannot find in Jewish tradition. The message of this book has been a simple one: when properly understood, Judaism has a coherent system of belief that fosters spiritual seriousness. Judaism offers a unique and distinctive way of life that makes "living the questions" compelling and rewarding. And it does all that while respecting our individuality and our intellectual integrity. There is no distinct mold into which a Jew must fit. We can participate in this tradition in many different ways, as very different sorts of people. That is why, as the quip has it, if you ask two Jews, you'll get three answers.

SO, THEN, WHAT IS JUDAISM?

If Judaism is so amorphous, does it really stand for anything? Is there a coherence to Jewish tradition? To Jewish belief?

Throughout this book, I have been arguing that the answer to those questions is yes. Let's review briefly what we have seen about what Judaism is and what Judaism has to offer.

THE DEMOCRATIZATION OF SPIRITUALITY

One of Judaism's most powerful claims is that its richness and profundity is accessible to everyone. It is not just for rabbis, for scholars, or for what some people call the "spiritual virtuoso" who has unique gifts. It tries to help all Jews, regardless of their age, intellectual disposition, background, or religious doubts, to sense God's presence in their lives.

Many of the rituals that Judaism now uses to sanctify in the home originated as part of a process of democratizing the priesthood. Instead of limiting the sacred to the domain of the Temple and the sphere of the priest, rabbinic tradition expanded Jewish ritual to make the sacred and the holy part of the daily lives of all Jews. While there may be a few people who can accomplish spiritual growth simply through introspection, the rabbis of the Talmud wanted that experience for everyone. They therefore opted for behavior in which everyone could participate. The multitude of rituals and practices that make up Jewish life, some of which have been discussed, all contribute to that goal.

Judaism's emphasis on study also furthered this goal of democratization. In one famous Talmudic passage, the rabbis clearly make the classic priesthood subservient to an emerging "priesthood" of study and knowledge. Speaking of which person should be ransomed first in the event that several are being held hostage, they wrote in the Mishnah:

> A Priest takes precedence over a Levite, a Levite over an Israelite, an Israelite over a bastard, a bastard over a Natin, a Natin over a proselyte, and a proselyte over an emancipated slave. This order of precedence applies only when all these were in other respects equal. If the bas-

tard, however, was a scholar and the High Priest an igno-
ramus, the learned bastard takes precedence over the ig-
norant High Priest.

(HORAYOT 13A)

Despite the importance normally accorded the priest, and especially the high priest, the process of study (accessible to all
Jews) had the potential to "trump" that genealogical advantage. The rabbis seem to have taken very seriously the Torah's
claim (Exodus 19:6) that Jews should be a "kingdom of priests
and a holy nation." The nation, and not just its leaders, are to
have access to the power and the wonder of religious life.

That is why in Jewish life the rabbi is a teacher, not an in-
termediary between the individual Jew and God. While in
some parts of the Christian tradition the priest plays such a
mediating role, Judaism sought direct access to God for each
Jew, without the rabbi as a go-between. The ways of life I have
been describing and the tradition of introspective study that is
so crucial to Judaism are designed to make that possible. They
assist us in creating moments for spiritual awareness and religious growth. They heighten our sensitivity to dimensions of
human life and of potential for sanctity that we might not
have previously sensed. The traditions that we have examined
about sexuality, food, time, and dress—parts of life that we inevitably take for granted on occasion—all serve this goal.
When we understand them fully, when we transcend the neg-
ative predispositions we sometimes have about Jewish tradition and ritual, we come to understand that Judaism's richness
is for everyone, its power accessible to all.

INTELLECTUAL SOPHISTICATION COUPLED WITH RELIGIOUS OPENNESS

Judaism therefore has a distinctly populist inclination; it seeks
to make its spiritual richness available to everyone who is interested in it. But at the same time, Judaism never sought to

achieve that accessibility by "lowering the stakes," by abandoning its intellectual sophistication. Indeed, it is precisely because some modern Jewish communities have failed to transmit Judaism's sophistication that they now face a crisis of Jewish identity. An educational system designed primarily to create affiliation without transmitting the substance and profundity of Jewish life has prompted Jews to ask, "Why Judaism?" Those communities in which children and adults are taught Jewish texts and tradition are communities in which Judaism's complex texture and sophistication are obvious and need no elaboration. To be sure, not everyone learns on the same level, and different people find different facets of Judaism's intellectualism appealing. But while some Jews believe that Judaism is merely a quaint ethnic way of life that has little to say about life's most important questions, we have seen that Judaism at its best is something very different.

Judaism is a tradition that celebrates intellectual rigor. There is nothing simple about the Talmud; its legal reasoning is as complex as any legal system. The worlds of *midrash* and *aggadah*, the stories the rabbis told to illustrate their religious claims, are complex literature. And the way that Jews study their tradition is designed to celebrate and accentuate the complexities of Jewish intellectual life, not to mask them. The Talmudic tradition speaks approvingly of "two scholars [studying together and] sharpening each other" (Shabbat 63a). Judaism is interested not in rote learning but in the use of the mind as a tool for the soul. Judaism asserts proudly that religious seriousness never needs to come at the expense of intellectual integrity or sophistication.

Yet Judaism's insistence on intellectual rigor never did away with its religious tolerance or openness. Judaism at its best has managed to balance intellectual sophistication, a deep respect for tradition and faith, and at the same time, a tolerance and understanding of the difficulties that faith often raises. This delicate balance is part of the wonder of Jewish life. Judaism is a religion that takes God very seriously, struggles to encounter a Force beyond us, worships God in daily life, prays to God (though as we saw, in ways that are dramatically different from what we commonly assume), and defines ethical behavior in terms of Godliness. And Jewish life is an intellectually sophisticated and open tradition that validates our struggle, legitimates our doubt. Judaism does not critique the person who doubts; it asks only that we continue the struggle, always seeking God's presence where it can be found.

This balance between intellectual rigor and the democracy of learning, between an insistence on study with an openness to questioning, is a difficult one. There are parts of the community where one element or another seems to overwhelm the other, to such an extent that Jewish tradition seems unidimensional. But this book has sought to show that, at its best, the tension is provocative, stimulating, and productive. The tension and the texture it produces for human life are one of the richest gifts Judaism has for those who explore it.

A WORLDLY TRADITION, WITH A MISSION

Another delicate balance: Although Judaism is a rich and technical intellectual tradition, it never divorced itself from the world, from a reality that desperately needs human involvement and creativity. Rabbi Jacob ben Asher's fourteenth-century legal code, the *Arba'ah Turim*, makes this point clearly. In a section that details the laws of study (including such technical matters as the age at which one must begin to teach children, what to teach them, what one must study later in life, who is eligible to teach, and the like), he concludes with the note that

> any learning which is unaccompanied by practical work
> is ultimately voided and leads to sin, for a person [who
> learns without working] robs humankind.
>
> (TUR YOREH DE'AH 245)

Judaism is not a religion of monasteries or of ascetics. Catholicism, to cite only one example, insisted that the priest be celibate as a sign of devotion to God; Jewish law, on the other hand, insisted that the cantor who represents the congregation on Yom Kippur be part of a family, and have children. Then and only then, the tradition asserts, can he share the community's sense of vulnerability and heartfelt need; only if he is part of the world in the fullest sense, Judaism believes, can he express the yearnings of the community he represents.

Traditional synagogues collect charity at each service that does not take place on a Shabbat or holiday (when money is not used). Even prayer, Jewish tradition asserts, has to have an impact on the world in an immediate way. Many of the rabbis in the Talmud, aside from their responsibilities as teachers and judges, also had trades. They were blacksmiths and woodchoppers, tradesmen and shopkeepers. Their intellectual pursuits were not a means of escaping the "real world." Similarly, a thousand years later, Maimonides worked as a physician. And today, the Israeli army has a program called *hesder*, which tailors the army schedules of young men who also wish to study in a *yeshiva* so that their program of study need not prevent them from serving in the military.

Jewish spirituality is not divorced from the world. Our discussion of Judaism's ethical tradition showed that the line between ritual and ethics in Jewish life is very fine, if it is discernible at all. God's command that Jews should be holy (Leviticus 19) is as much a manifesto for the repair of the world as it is a program for the healing of the soul. Jewish life is life with a mission: to grow religiously, to question life's meaning, and to leave the world a better place than we found it. A famous Talmudic story about dreaming makes the point:

> R. Johanan said: A righteous man named Honi was troubled throughout his life about the meaning of the verse, "A Song of Ascents, When the Lord brought back those

that returned to Zion, we were like unto them that dream" (Psalms 126:1). [He wondered]: Is it possible for a man to dream continuously for seventy years [the length of the Jewish exile after the destruction of the First Temple]?

One day he was journeying on the road and he saw a man planting a carob tree. He asked him, "How long does it take [for this tree] to bear fruit?" The man replied: "Seventy years." He then further asked him: "Are you certain that you will live another seventy years?" The man replied: "I found [ready-grown] carob trees in the world; as my forefathers planted these for me so I too plant these for my children."

(TA'ANIT 23A)

That, too, Judaism insists, was a religious act. Environmentalism and human rights are not substitutes for religious seriousness, nor are they diversions from it. They are part of its essence. Jewish life does not demand a choice between social activism, political passion, and religious seriousness. Judaism is a tradition that validates all, and believes that each informs and enriches the other.

WHAT REALLY MATTERS?
Finally, we can put the matter somewhat differently. Jewish life is ultimately about asking, "What really matters?" What are the sorts of relationships that make life richly lived? What are the causes that deserve our attention? What do we believe is "out there"? What do we need to do to assure ourselves that once we are gone, our lives will not have been wasted?

These are profound questions, and they do not lend themselves to easy answers. Indeed, more important than the answers may be the processes of asking and wondering. That is why the metaphor of the journey is so important to Jewish life.

Judaism understands that no one wants to struggle forever. It understands that there are few people who can contemplate these questions on an ongoing basis. But it insists that the questions are important. So it weaves these questions into a unique way of life that offers community and connection, joy and comfort, study and celebration, and that in the process enriches our lives by beckoning to us and helping us to ask the questions that frame our most important decisions.

The Talmud expresses this idea in the following powerful passage:

> Raba said: When a person [dies, they are] led in for Judgment and asked: Did you engage in business dealings faithfully [i.e., with integrity], did you fix times for learning, did you engage in procreation, did you hope for salvation, did you engage in the dialectics of wisdom, did you understand one thing from another?
>
> (SHABBAT 31A)

It is not entirely clear what Raba intended by each of these questions. The meaning of the last two in particular has been the subject of much debate. But this list of six questions that Raba suggests we will be asked upon our deaths (or more likely, the questions he felt we should use to guide our lives) make certain priorities clear. The first question is about ethics. If we were not decent, ethical people, nothing else matters. And Judaism is designed to help sharpen our ethical sensitivity and awareness.

But Raba suggests that decency is not enough. The examined life, he suggests, is available to all. Everyone needs to set aside time for the study of Torah, and (according to at least one reading of the final two questions) must use their intellectual skills to draw their own conclusions about life's important questions. Perhaps most interestingly, the tradition refuses to accept despair. It commands us to have children if we are able, and even insists that we are obliged to hope for salvation!

What a strange but wonderful approach to spirituality. An emphasis on morality and intellectualism. A seriousness about spirituality and searching. And an insistence on optimism, joy, and hope. If Jews experienced Judaism in that way more often, would they turn away? If that were the Judaism that modern Jews had been brought up with, would they have had any trouble explaining why having a *bris* for their sons or a *simḥat bat* for their daughters is important? There is a richness and power to Jewish life that speaks for itself, if only Jews will let it.

But many modern Jews did not grow up with Judaism explained in this light. And yet, they do not wish to give up. How to start? How do we begin? Is it ever too late? What are the very first steps to take?

BEGINNING A JEWISH SPIRITUAL ODYSSEY

The mere idea of beginning a Jewish spiritual odyssey seems daunting to many people. Because there is so much to master, Jews often fear that it may be too late for them to begin. But Jewish tradition asserts that it is never too late. Indeed, in celebrating the life and accomplishments of one of the greatest rabbinic authorities of all time, Rabbi Akiba, it insists that late beginnings are never an obstacle to great accomplishment. The Talmud tells the following story about Rabbi Akiba and his unique path to Jewish learning:

> R. Akiba was a shepherd of Ben Kalba Sabua. The latter's daughter, seeing how modest and noble [the shepherd]

was, said to him, "Were I to be betrothed to you, would you go away to [study at] an academy?" "Yes," he replied. She was then secretly betrothed to him and sent him away. When her father heard [what she had done] he drove her from his house and forbade her by a vow to have any benefit from his estate.

[R. Akiba] departed and spent twelve years at the academy. When he returned home he brought with him twelve thousand disciples. [While in his hometown] he heard an old man saying to her, "How long will you lead the life of a living widowhood?" "If he would listen to me," she replied, "he would spend [in study] another twelve years." Said [R. Akiba to himself]: "It is then with her consent that I am acting," and he departed again and spent another twelve years at the academy.

When he finally returned he brought with him twenty-four thousand disciples. His wife heard [of his arrival] and went out to meet him, when her neighbors said to her, "Borrow some respectable clothes and put them on," but she replied: "A righteous man regardeth the life of his beast" (Proverbs 12:10). On approaching him she fell upon her face and kissed his feet. His attendants were about to thrust her aside, when [R. Akiba] cried to them, "Leave her alone, mine and yours are hers."

Her father, on hearing that a great man had come to the town, said, "I shall go to him; perchance he will invalidate my vow." When he came to him [R. Akiba] asked, "Would you have made your vow if you had known that he was a great man?" "[Had he known]," the other replied, "even one chapter or even one single halakhah [I would not have made the vow]." He then said to him, "I am the one." The other fell upon his face and kissed his feet and also gave him half of his wealth.

(KETUBBOT 62B–63A)

What was the key to Rabbi Akiba's rise from the status of a simple shepherd to that of a renowned scholar? A devotion to learning. Indeed, this charming Talmudic story is a story of many devotions. Of Rachel's and Akiba's devotion to each other, her devotion to his mind and his intellectual potential, and his passion for learning. With devotion and passion, the tradition asserts, even late beginnings can be overcome. Indeed, another tradition, also about Rabbi Akiba, claims that his life was divided into three distinct phases: for the first forty years he labored as a shepherd, for the next forty years he studied, and for the last forty years of his life, he taught (*Sifrei Ve-Zot Ha-Berakhah*). Even Rabbi Akiba began late. Despite all there is to know about Jewish life, and despite the fact that, as we have seen, it is knowledge and understanding that are key to sensing Judaism's great spiritual power, it is never too late to begin.

WHY JUDAISM?

At the very outset of this book, I pointed to a simple question that many Jews have begun to ask. Why have a *bris* for a newborn son? But that question, as was noted, is not really a question about a *bris*. It is a question about Jewish life, a question that modern Jews constantly confront. Jews today struggle with the question "Why be Jewish?" because they have never been exposed to the power and spirituality of Jewish living. Through no fault of their own, they have no sophisticated sense of what Judaism has to offer.

But Jewish life, I have sought to demonstrate, has the potential to be a rich and satisfying way of living. It offers a combination of qualities that are difficult to find anywhere else. But these qualities, for all that I have tried to describe them, are better experienced than discussed. Jewish life, like music, defies adequate explanation. People who love music cannot put their love into words, nor can they describe what playing or listening to music does for them. Jewish life, too, is a matter as much of the heart and soul as of the intellect. Ultimately, the question "Why be Jewish?" cannot be satisfactorily answered with words alone. Jewish life has to be experienced. Its power, its majesty, its sensitivity, and its wisdom come alive to Jews when they live it, not when they simply think about it. This book has been an attempt to point to the fundamental elements of Jewish life that have spiritual power and potential. But how well could one describe in words the sound of a flute, a harp, a violin?

Is Judaism the only way to embark on a spiritual quest? Certainly not. Then why Judaism? Because, as we have seen, Judaism is a sophisticated and subtle tradition that has spoken to Jews for thousands of years. Because it still speaks to Jews who explore it and make it part of their lives. Because it is who we are. It is our home. It tells not just a story, but the story of our family, our history, our people. To live as a Jew is to join our ancestors in their mission. To make their mission into ours. To live as a Jew is to chart a course for our children, and theirs. It is to live as part of something larger than we are—a nation, a people, a historical community. To live as a Jew is to place ourselves in a context, with God, history, Torah, and the Jewish people at our sides and as our guides.

In quiet, vulnerable moments, we admit to ourselves that we cannot live forever. We will die, leaving the world for those who come after us. Will we have lived well? Will our lives have mattered? Will our successes and sorrows have had meaning? Judaism offers us a chance to say yes. It offers us a chance to join something important, something noble. Something that can tie us to generations of our family long ago, and generations we still cannot imagine. It offers us a chance to ask life's most important questions, and to join with other human beings in living our limited days richly, thoughtfully, and ethically, so that at the dusk of life we will be able to look back with satisfaction, with confidence, and even with hope.

GLOSSARY OF HEBREW NAMES AND TERMS

◇

THE FOLLOWING IS A LIST OF HEBREW NAMES AND JEWISH TERMS that appear throughout the book. The definitions that follow are not technical definitions but popular ones, designed only to assist the reader in understanding this book.

Adon Olam: "Lord of the world," a liturgical poem commonly recited before going to sleep and at the conclusion of Sabbath morning services.

aggadah: a genre of stories told by the rabbis of the rabbinic period to make theological, ethical, and religious claims.

ahavat yisrael: Hebrew phrase meaning "the love of Israel," generally referring to "the love of one's fellow Jews."

Akedah: Hebrew term for the episode in the book of Genesis known as "the Binding of Isaac."

Amalek: ancient people mentioned in the Torah as a group that attacked the Israelites on their journey from Egypt to the Promised Land. The Torah commands that the Jews blot out the memory of the Amalek.

Amidah: the central prayer of the Jewish liturgy. The weekday version (as opposed to versions for Sabbath and holidays) is also known as the *Shemoneh Esrei,* or the *Eighteen Benedictions.* In much of rabbinic literature, the *Amidah* is also called *ha-tefillah,* or " the prayer."

am kadosh: Hebrew phrase meaning "holy nation." The Hebrew can also mean "separate nation."

Arba'ah Turim: the name of a fourteenth-century religious code of Jewish law. The name means "the four pillars."

Berikh Shemei: "Blessed Is God's Name," a portion of the prayer book recited as the Torah is removed from the ark on Shabbat morning.

bris: the colloquial term used to refer to a ritual circumcision, usually performed on the eighth day of a Jewish boy's life.

challah: a special bread, usually a braided egg bread, eaten as part of Sabbath and Festival meals.

Elohai Nezor: the first words of the final paragraph of the *Amidah.* The full phrase means "my God, keep my tongue from evil."

Ethics of the Fathers: a tractate of the Mishnah, also called *Pirkei Avot* in Hebrew, which contains sayings and religious-ethical teachings from the third century B.C.E to the third century C.E.

Gaon of Vilna: Elijah ben Solomon Zalman (1720–1797). A Lithuanian talmudist renowned for his intellect and piety.

Haggadah: a rabbinic text that narrates the story of the exodus from Egypt. It is recited in the home on Passover at a traditional meal called a Seder.

Haman: villain of the Purim story, recounted in the Biblical book of Esther. According to tradition, he plotted to have the Jewish community of Persia murdered.

Hanukkah: an eight-day winter holiday celebrating the rededication of the Temple in Jerusalem after it was recaptured from the Greeks by the Hasmoneans. Today it is celebrated with a variety of rituals, the most well known of which is the lighting of the Hanukkah candles.

hasidei umot ha-olam: a Hebrew phrase, commonly translated as "righteous gentiles," often to refer to those non-Jews who helped save Jews during times of grave threat to the Jewish people. Literally, the phrase means "the righteous ones of the nations of the earth."

Hasidic: belonging to or stemming from the Jewish community that had its roots in the pietistic movement started by Israel Baal Shem Tov (1699–1761).

ha-tefillah: a Hebrew word that literally means "the prayer." In rabbinical literature, this word is often used to refer to the *Amidah.*

Havdalah: a Hebrew word meaning "separation." It is often used to refer to the ceremony that concludes the Sabbath.

havruta: an Aramaic word that generally refers to a Torah study partner.

he'emin: a Hebrew word meaning "believed" or "trusted." The Torah uses this word to describe Abraham's faith in God.

hesder: a program in the Israeli army that tailors the schedule of army service to the needs of young men who also wish to study in a *yeshiva*.

huppah: the traditional Jewish wedding canopy.

Ima Shalom: One of the relatively few women mentioned in the Talmud, she was known as a virtuous person who encouraged her husband, Eliezer ben Hyrcanus, to engage in study. She lived in the first century C.E.

Itturei Torah: a Hebrew phrase that literally means "crowns of the Torah." It is a twentieth-century anthology and interpretation of classical commentaries on the Torah.

kabbalists: a term for Jewish mystics, descendants of a group that had its roots in sixteenth-century Palestinian Jewish communities.

Kaddish: A Jewish prayer recited by mourners that praises and sanctifies God's name.

kashrut: a Hebrew term that refers to the body of Jewish dietary laws.

kavvanah: a Hebrew word that means "intention."

kedushah: a Hebrew word that means "holiness" or "separateness."

ketubbah: the Jewish marriage document, the signing and reading of which is an integral part of traditional Jewish wedding ceremonies.

keva: a Hebrew word that means "fixed." It is commonly used to refer to the formulaic element of Jewish prayer.

Kiddush: a Hebrew word meaning "sanctification." It generally refers to a prayer recited Friday evening and Saturday morning that sanctifies the Sabbath day. It is recited over a goblet of wine.

kippah: Hebrew for yarmulkah.

Kizzur Shulhan Arukh: an abridgment of Judaism's major law code prepared by Rabbi Solomon Ganzfried in 1863.

lekh-lekha: a Hebrew phrase meaning "go forth!" It appears in Genesis 12:1, and is part of the first words that God speaks to Abram, the first Jew.

Maccabees: the Jewish troops who fought the Greek occupiers of ancient Judea during the second century B.C.E. Their successful recapturing of the Temple led to the creation of the holiday of Hanukkah.

Maimonides: Judaism's most important philosopher, he lived from 1135 to 1204. He also composed the *Thirteen Principles of Faith*.

mash-ber': a Hebrew word meaning "crisis." It was also used to refer to a birthing stool used by women in ancient times.

mezuzah: a small ritual object that is affixed to door posts and contains sacred texts inside.

midrash: a Hebrew term that means "exploration" or "investigation." It generally refers to rabbinic narratives or homilies that explore scriptural sources for additional insight and meaning.

Midrash Tanhuma: a compilation of rabbinic homilies and interpretations attributed to Rabbi Tanhuma bar Abba, of the late fourth century.

mikveh: a Hebrew term for a ritual bath.

minyan: a Hebrew word that literally means "counting"; it is generally used to refer to the prayer quorum of ten Jewish adults.

Mishnah: The earliest major document of Rabbinic Judaism, it was compiled by Rabbi Judah the Patriarch in approximately 220 C.E.

mitzvah: a Hebrew word that means "commandment."

mohel: a Hebrew word that refers to the person who performs a ritual circumcision.

Natin: a person of Gibeonite ancestry; not considered full-fledged members of the Jewish people.

Passover Seder: a ritual meal commemorating the exodus from Egypt. The central feature of this meal is the recitation of the *Haggadah*.

Raba: the name of a Talmudic scholar, usually Rabbah bar Nahmani, who lived in the third and fourth centuries in Babylonia.

Rabban Gamaliel: the name of several Palestinian rabbis. Rabban Gamaliel II, who lived toward the end of the first century C.E., was known for his keen intellect and political power.

Rabbi Akiba: the frequently used name of Akiba ben Joseph, c. 50–135 C.E. of Judea. He was among the foremost creators of the Talmudic tradition.

Rabbi Eleazar Azikri: a medieval Jewish poet, he lived from 1533 to 1600. He was the author of *Yedid Nefesh*, a liturgical composition recited Friday evening in the synagogue at the beginning of Sabbath services.

Rabbi Eliezer: a rabbinic sage of the late first century C.E..

Rabbi Haninah: a first-century Palestinian rabbinic scholar.

Rabbi Jacob ben Asher: A Jewish legal scholar who lived from 1269 to 1340. He wrote the *Arba'ah Turim*, one of Judaism's most important legal codes.

Rabbi Judah the Patriarch: a second-century C.E. Palestinian Jewish scholar who is credited with the codification of the Mishnah in the year 220 C.E.

rabbinic literature: a term used to refer to Judaism's oral tradition, a compilation that began approximately 250 years before the common era and continued until the sixth century C.E. It includes the Mishnah, Talmud, *midrash*, and other works.

Rachel: a common name for Jewish women, it was also the name of Rabbi Akiba's wife.

Rashi: an acronym for Rabbi Solomon ben Isaac of Troyes (1040–1105), perhaps the greatest Jewish commentator on the Bible and Talmud.

Rav: an early-third-century C.E. rabbinic authority.

Rav Huna: a rabbinic authority of the third century C.E.

Rosh Ha-Shanah: the Jewish holiday that commemorates the beginning of a new Jewish year.

Rosh Ḥodesh: the beginning of the Jewish month, tied to the lunar cycle.

Samuel: a Babylonian rabbinic authority who lived from the end of the second century C.E. to the middle of the third century C.E.

Seder plate: a ritual object used on Passover to display the ritual foods used as part of the recounting of the story of the Exodus from Egypt.

Shabbat Zakhor: the Sabbath immediately preceding the holiday of Purim. On this day Jews read a special selection from the Torah about the tribe of Amalek, who attacked the Jews on their way from Egypt to the Promised Land.

Shavuot: the "Festival of Weeks" that celebrates the giving of the law by God to the Jewish people at Mount Sinai. It falls seven weeks and one day after the beginning of Passover.

Shema: a Hebrew word that means "listen," it is also the name of a central element of the Jewish liturgy. The specific phrase comes from Deuteronomy 6:4.

Sheva Berakhot: a Hebrew phrase which means "seven blessings," it generally refers to the seven marital blessings recited under the wedding canopy as part of the wedding ceremony.

Shimon ben Yochai: mid-second-century Palestinian rabbi. A pupil of Rabbi Akiba, he is traditionally credited with having written the Zohar, a classic mystical Jewish work.

Shoah: a Hebrew word meaning "calamity," or "devastation," it is the term for the Nazi Holocaust.

shtibl: a Yiddish word for a small, informal synagogue.

shul: a Yiddish word for "synagogue."

siddur: a Hebrew word meaning "order," it is commonly used to refer to the Jewish prayer book.

simḥat bat: a relatively modern Jewish ceremony for naming girls and formally bringing them into the covenant between the Jewish people and God.

Simḥat Torah: the Jewish holiday that celebrates the Jewish people's study of Torah, it coincides with the annual completion of the cycle of reading the entire Torah.

Solomon ibn Gabirol: A Spanish Jewish poet and philosopher who lived from 1021 to 1058.

Song of Songs: The name of one of the books of the Bible. A graphic love poem, it was seen by the rabbinic tradition as a metaphor for God's love for Israel.

Sukkot: a holiday known as the "Festival of Booths." It takes place in the fall and commemorates the experience of the Jewish people in the desert when they lived in temporary, unstable dwellings.

tallit: a Jewish prayer shawl, worn by men (and today, by some women as well) during morning prayers.

Talmud: a Hebrew word meaning "teaching," it is generally used to refer to the Babylonian Talmud, rabbinic Judaism's greatest compendium of legal and ethical teachings.

talmud torah: a Hebrew phrase that means "the study of Torah."

tefillin: an Aramaic word used to refer to phylacteries, the leather boxes and leather straps that contain Biblical passages inscribed on parchment and are worn on the forehead and arm during morning prayer.

Temple: the central Jewish location of worship and sacrifice in ancient Jerusalem.

Torah: a Hebrew word that means "teaching," it commonly refers to the Five Books of Moses, the first five books of the Hebrew Bible.

Tosafists *or* Tosafot: medieval Jewish European legal authorities and commentators on the Talmud.

tzeddakah: a Hebrew word that means "righteousness" or "justice," it is the term commonly used for the giving of charity.

Yedid Nefesh: a Hebrew phrase meaning "Beloved Companion." It is the name of a poem sung at the beginning of Sabbath services on Friday evening.

Yehuda Ha-Levi: A Spanish Jewish poet and philosopher who lived from 1085 to 1140.

yeshiva: a Hebrew word for academies of traditional Jewish learning.

yisrael: "Israel" in English, it is a Hebrew word that comes from a phrase meaning "to struggle with God."

Yizhak: Hebrew for the name Isaac.

Yom Kippur: a Hebrew phrase that means "the day of atonement," it is a Jewish holiday that falls the week after Rosh Ha-Shanah and is commonly considered the holiest day of the year. On this day Jews repent their sins and seek the strength to live better lives during the upcoming year.

zemirot: a Hebrew word for special songs written for the Sabbath.

Zohar: the central text of Kabbalah, or Jewish mysticism. Despite a tradition that claims it was composed by Rabbi Shimon bar Yochai, it was apparently largely written by Moses de Leon in the 1280s.

Suggestions for Further Reading

◇

As interest in Jewish life and culture has intensified over the past several decades, dozens of wonderful and insightful books have appeared on a variety of topics related to Judaism. The following lists suggest only a few of those that touch on the topics of each of the chapters. There are many other superb volumes not included here, but these should provide at least a place to begin.

INTRODUCTION: THE CRISIS AND THE OPPORTUNITY

Kosmin, Barry A., et al. *Highlights of the CFJ 1990 National Jewish Population Survey* (New York: Council of Jewish Federations, 1991).

Silberman, Charles C. *A Certain People: American Jews and Their Lives Today* (New York: Summit Books, 1985). An argument that anti-Jewish sentiment in America is at an all-time low. Silberman's conclusions about the Jewish future are dubious, but his data and his analysis remain thoughtful and worth reading.

CHAPTER ONE: JUDAISM AS A SPIRITUAL ODYSSEY

Cowan, Paul. *An Orphan in History: Retrieving a Jewish Legacy* (Garden City, N.Y.: Doubleday, 1982). An account of Cowan's odyssey as he rediscovers his Jewish roots and finds new religious meaning and energy in a Judaism he had never taken seriously. An eminently readable and deeply compelling personal statement.

Dershowitz, Alan. *Chutzpah* (Boston: Little, Brown, 1991). Dershowitz's controversial but important thesis is that American Jews are much more secure in this country than they imagine, and that American Jews need not constantly worry about how non-Jewish Americans will view their behavior. American Jews, he argues, need more *chutzpah*, or audacity. A compelling advocacy for Jewish self-confidence in America.

Funkenstein, Amos. *Perceptions of Jewish History* (Berkeley: University of California Press, 1993). Funkenstein's book is an implicit rebuttal of Yerushalmi's book, listed below. Both Funkenstein and Yerushalmi, giants in the field of Jewish history, are interested in the power of Jewish memory. This is an academic book, but is well worth reading despite the occasionally difficult sections.

Kushner, Lawrence. *Honey from the Rock: Visions of Jewish Mystical Renewal* (New York: Harper and Row, 1977). A beautiful, almost poetic book about spirituality in the world of Jewish life. Much of the book focuses on prayer, but in the opening sections the reader finds some of the best descriptions of what spirituality is.

Yerushalmi, Yosef Hayim. *Zakhor: Jewish History and Jewish Memory* (New York: Schocken Books, 1982). A scholarly but approachable analysis of how memory works in Jewish life. Very stimulating, though a little difficult. A classic for those interested in pursuing the issues of nostalgia and memory raised in this chapter.

CHAPTER TWO: JUDAISM AND BELIEF IN GOD

Dorff, Elliot. *Knowing God* (Northvale, N.J.: Jason Aronson, 1992). A personal statement by one of Conservative Judaism's most important personalities, this volume is accessible to the lay reader and does an excellent job of introducing Judaism's most important and enduring theological arguments.

Gordis, Robert. *A Faith for Moderns* (New York: Bloch Publishing Company, 1971). Somewhat dated, this volume nonetheless remains one of the finest modern rationalist arguments for God and Judaism. For committed rationalists, the section on God will be very helpful.

Heschel, Abraham Joshua. *Man Is Not Alone: A Philosophy of Religion* (Philadelphia: Jewish Publication Society of America, 1951). Heschel was one of the most important Jewish thinkers of the twentieth century, and by far the most poetic. This book is not merely *about* spirituality; reading it is a spiritual experience.

Holtz, Barry W., ed. *Back to the Sources: Reading the Classic Jewish Texts* (New York: Summit Books, 1984). An excellent anthology (see discussion for Chapter Three); the chapter on *midrash* discusses the *midrashic* selections found in this chapter, and offers lovely explanations of them.

Steinberg, Milton. *Basic Judaism* (New York and London: Harcourt, Brace, Jovanovich, 1947). Probably the finest statement on the essence of Judaism, this brief and readable volume has an excellent section on God.

Telushkin, Joseph. *Jewish Literacy* (New York: William Morrow, 1991). This book contains 346 very brief chapters that trace Jewish history and ideas from the very beginning to the present. People interested in building a solid Jewish knowledge base appreciate the brevity of the chapters, allowing the reader to work through several pages each day without stopping in the middle of a chapter. The superb index also allows the book to serve as a mini-encyclopedia of Jewish life.

Wolpe, David. *In Speech and In Silence* (New York: Henry Holt, 1992). Mentioned in the list for Chapter Three as well, this volume deserves mention here especially as it relates to the theme of silence explored in this chapter.

CHAPTER THREE: JEWISH "CONVERSATIONS" AND THE WRITTEN WORD

Biale, David. *Power and Powerlessness in Jewish Tradition* (New York: Schocken Books, 1986). A historical study of Jewish history and the ways in which Jewish communities created and used unique types of power to suit their unique circumstances. Biale's discussion of the rabbinic community's turn to the power of words (primarily the first three chapters) is relevant to the discussion of this chapter.

Holtz, Barry W., ed. *Back to the Sources: Reading the Classic Jewish Texts* (New York: Summit Books, 1984). Considered the classic volume for newcomers to the world of Jewish text. Each chapter, written by a different scholar, introduces the layperson to a different genre of Jewish writing. There are no better introductions.

Kaufman, Yehezkiel. *The Religion of Israel: From the Babylonian Captivity to the End of Prophecy* (New York: Ktav Publishing House, 1976). A classic description of biblical religion. In the very final pages, Kaufman sets the stage for a transition to postbiblical Judaism, and introduces the notion of the portability of Jewish texts.

Neusner, Jacob. *Ancient Israel After Catastrophe: The Religious World View of the Mishnah* (Charlottesville: University Press of Virginia, 1983). A brilliant and very brief articulation of Neusner's thesis that the Mishnah is a reaction to the chaos introduced into Jewish life by the Romans' destruction of the Temple. A very compelling analysis of the religious worldview of the Mishnah, in a few succinct and readable chapters. An excellent insight into the role of text in the Jewish psyche.

Ochs, Vanessa L. *Words on Fire: One Woman's Journey into the Sacred* (San Diego: Harcourt, Brace, Jovanovich, 1990). An insightful and self-aware account of an American woman's first serious encounter with the study of Jewish texts in Jerusalem. Of interest not only to women concerned with a uniquely female approach to these texts, but to everyone curious about the power the traditional world of learning has for its adherents.

Wolpe, David. *In Speech and In Silence: The Jewish Quest for God* (New York: Henry Holt, 1992). A powerful series of meditations on the subjects of speech and silence as Jews struggle to sense the sublime. Wolpe somehow bridges the worlds of prose and poetry. A beautiful, moving personal expression of the poetic in Jewish religious life.

CHAPTER FOUR: RITUAL

The Complete Artscroll Siddur. (New York: Mesorah Publications, 1984). A prayer book produced by the Orthodox community, this edition contains the full text of almost all major Jewish rituals, and a very literal translation for those who wish to study the rituals in detail.

Geffen, Rela M., ed. *Celebration and Renewal: Rites of Passage in Judaism* (Philadelphia: Jewish Publication Society of America, 1993). A collection of essays on the major stages of the Jewish cycle, explaining the rituals that take place at each stage, their origins, and the meaning and symbolism of each. Each of the authors takes a slightly different approach, but there are many fine essays in the volume.

Greenberg, Blu. *How to Run a Traditional Jewish Household* (Northvale, N.J.: Jason Aronson, 1993). Greenberg writes both as a feminist and as an Orthodox Jew. This is one of the finest introductions to the many rituals that are part of Jewish home life, written with sensitivity, wisdom, and an inviting style.

Greenberg, Irving. *The Jewish Way: Living the Holidays* (New York: Simon & Schuster, 1988). While there are a number of "how-to" books about the Jewish holidays, none comes close to this one in explaining in thoughtful and sophisticated language the meaning behind them and the spiritual beauty of the Jewish calendar year.

Heschel, Abraham Joshua. *The Sabbath: Its Meaning for Modern Man* (New York: Farrar, Straus and Young, 1951). A classic, this brief book is the most poetic statement about the meaning of Shabbat written in the modern period. The beauty of its imagery consistently moves both newcomers to Jewish ritual as well as those who have long participated in it.

Ives, Robert. *Shabbat and Festival Shiron* (Beverly Hills, Calif.: Robert Ives, 1992). This small book contains the full text, in Hebrew, English, and transliterations, of the prayers and songs for the Shabbat table. Its brief explanations are also helpful, especially for newcomers to the Shabbat traditions.

Neusner, Jacob. *Ancient Israel After Catastrophe: The Religious World View of the Mishnah* (Charlottesville: University Press of Virginia, 1983). Neusner is by far the most prolific student of ancient Judaism today. This small volume is an insightful reading of the Mishnah, demonstrating how a book of law and ritual responded to the spiritual and psychological needs of the Jewish people in the aftermath of the Temple's destruction.

Strassfeld, Michael, and Sharon Strassfeld. *The Jewish Catalogue: Volumes I, II, and III* (Philadelphia: Jewish Publication Society of America, 1973, 1976, and 1980). Products of the 1960s revival in Jewish spirituality, these paperback volumes have become classics. They contain excellent introductions to countless Jewish rituals, combining humor, wisdom, and much practical advice. Though slightly dated stylistically, they remain excellent both for reference and for getting started in Jewish ritual life.

Wolfson, Ronald. *The Art of Jewish Living: The Shabbat Seder* (1985), *The Passover Seder* (1988), *Hanukkah* (1990), *A Time to Mourn, A Time to Comfort* (1993) (New York: The Federation of Jewish Men's Clubs and the University of Judaism). Wolfson's books are the best of the "how-to" genre on those holidays and life-cycle events he has covered. They are highly readable, accurate, and provide an excellent introduction for people interested in learning how to participate in these various rituals.

CHAPTER FIVE: *MITZVAH* AS COMMANDMENT

Berkovitz, Eliezer. *Not in Heaven: The Nature and Function of Halakhah* (New York: Ktav Publishing House, 1983). Perhaps the finest liberal Orthodox discussion of *halakhah*, and one of the few Orthodox works to take seriously possible conflicts between Jewish law and morality.

Gillman, Neil. *Sacred Fragments: Recovering Theology for the Modern Jew* (Philadelphia: Jewish Publication Society of America, 1990). Gillman's book takes the reader through all the major questions that developing a personal theology entails, and helps elucidate what others have said and what is at stake. A superb volume. Chapter Two, entitled "Religious Authority: Who Commands?" will be invaluable to Jews interested in pursuing the theology of *mitzvah*.

Hartman, David. *A Living Covenant* (New York: The Free Press, 1985). A modern Orthodox rabbi, keenly aware of the critiques leveled against unrestrained submission, argues poetically and effectively that such is not the intention of Jewish tradition. He deals extensively with the work of Yeshayahu Leibowitz, quoted in this chapter. Difficult in places, but well worth the effort.

Kadushin, Max. *The Rabbinic Mind* (New York: Bloch Publishing Company, 1965). Kadushin introduces the concept of "normal mysticism," arguing that everyday Jewish life is designed to make certain elements of mystical, profoundly spiritual life part of the daily regimen of Jews. Deeply thoughtful, and while more sophisticated than many popular works, it is still eminently readable.

Kaplan, Mordecai M. *Judaism as a Civilization* (Philadelphia: Jewish Publication Society of America, 1981). The classic statement of what is now called Reconstructionist Judaism by the thinker who inspired and created the movement. A classic.

Neusner, Jacob. *Ancient Israel After Catastrophe: The Religious World View of the Mishnah* (Charlottesville: University Press of Virginia, 1983). Neusner, an important explicator of the rabbinic tradition, makes an interesting argument that much of rabbinic law is a response to the emotional setting in which early Jews found themselves. Readers interested in further thinking on plausibility structures will enjoy this very brief but provocative work.

————. *A Rabbi Talks to Jesus: An Intermillennial, Interfaith Exchange* (New York: Doubleday, 1993). Neusner invents a conversation that he might have had with Jesus had he been present at the Sermon on the Mount, in order to explain why he believes Jews could not accept Jesus' teachings. A very readable, clever, and interesting book.

Roth, Joel. *The Halakhic Process* (New York: Jewish Theological Seminary of America, 1986). A technical and very difficult work, Roth's book is an excellent summary of how Jewish law works and how law in Judaism evolves. It has been critiqued for its commitment to a philosophy known as legal positivism, but is still an exceedingly valuable contribution to the field.

CHAPTER SIX: PRAYER

The Complete Artscroll Siddur (New York: Mesorah Publications, 1984). A prayer book produced by the Orthodox community, this has some distinct advantages. The English translation, while not particularly poetic, is literal, and thus provides an excellent sense of what the original means. This prayer book also has complete instructions on how and when to recite the prayer, and a listing of the verses associated with individuals' Hebrew names.

Donin, Hayim Halevi. *To Pray as a Jew: A Guide to the Prayerbook and the Synagogue Service* (New York: Basic Books, 1980). An excellent introduction to the structure and customs of Jewish prayer, from a mainstream Orthodox perspective. Part of a series that includes *To Live as a Jew* and *To Raise a Jewish Child*.

Dorff, Elliot. *Knowing God* (Northvale, N.J.: Jason Aronson, 1992). Chapter Six, "Knowing God Through Human Words," is the primary section that addresses the liturgy. Dorff's analogy of prayer to baseball is one of the most creative sections of the book and is well worth noting.

Hammer, Reuven. *Entering Jewish Prayer* (New York: Schocken Books, 1994). The newest full-volume introduction to the structure of the service and its spiritual content. A very thoughtful and sensitive introduction to the world of Jewish prayer.

Jacobson, B. S. *Meditations on the Siddur: Studies in the Essential Problems and Ideas of Jewish Worship* (Tel Aviv: Sinai Publishing, 1978). A highly detailed and scholarly discussion of Jewish prayer, and of many individual prayers. Based on the Hebrew *Netiv Binah*, this is a volume of impressive scholarship, but one that is still accessible to relative beginners as well. Not easy reading, but worth the try.

———. *The Weekday Siddur: An Exposition and Analysis of Its Structure, Contents, Language and Ideas* (Tel Aviv: Sinai Publishing, 1978). Similar to the above, but concentrating on the liturgy of the weekday prayer book.

Millgram, Abraham E. *Jewish Worship* (Philadelphia: Jewish Publication Society of America, 1971). A useful and readable introduction to the world of Jewish prayer. The most modern of the general introductions listed here.

CHAPTER SEVEN: JEWISH ETHICS

Gordis, Robert. *Judaic Ethics for a Lawless World* (New York: Jewish Theological Seminary of America, 1986). An interesting argument that a major thrust of Jewish life is the goal of providing ethical standards for an otherwise lawless world. This book is accessible to the lay reader and provides important background to Judaism's attitudes to many different ethical dilemmas.

Kellner, Menachem. *Contemporary Jewish Ethics* (New York: Sanhedrin Press, 1979). Unlike the volume discussed above, this is an edited work, with essays by radically differing Jewish writers and thinkers on many of the most commonly discussed ethical issues, including capital punishment, medical ethics, and the like. There are now many books in this genre, but this volume has stood the test of time.

Lerner, Michael. *Jewish Renewal* (New York: G.P. Putnam's Sons, 1994). Michael Lerner began his Jewish career as a radical of the 1960s. A quarter of a century later, this is his major manifesto and "call to arms," which argues that Judaism is about radically transforming the world and eradicating pain and cruelty from human society. The book reflects a rather "left-wing" reading of both Judaism and politics, but is well worth reading regardless of one's personal perspective.

Neusner, Jacob. *Tzeddakah* (Chappaqua, N.Y.: Rossel Books, 1982). This is a very short book that serves as an interesting introduction to the Jewish tradition of charity. One of its most important elements, found at the end of the book, is a long series of quotations of original sources on the subject, which are also translated into English. As always, Neusner takes a familiar topic and reads it in an interesting new light.

Potok, Chaim. *Ethical Living for a Modern World: Jewish Insights* (New York: Jewish Theological Seminary of America, 1985). A typescript of a series of pamphlets that Potok wrote on ethical issues, this informal volume presents an extraordinary array of original source material, and some interesting ways of addressing it.

Schulweis, Harold M. *Evil and the Morality of God* (Cincinnati: Hebrew Union College Press, 1984). Schulweis, a Conservative rabbi who follows largely in the Reconstructionist tradition of Rabbi Mordecai Kaplan, addresses the timeless question of good and evil. He argues that ultimately we cannot say "God is . . ." All we can say is that "Godliness is . . ." This is a very difficult book, but worth the effort because of the challenging and innovative claims that it makes.

Spero, Shubert. *Morality, Halakhah and the Jewish Tradition* (New York: Ktav Publishing House, 1983). Written from a rather traditional perspective, this is still one of the best summaries of the place of ethics in the Jewish legal tradition. It is complete, accessible, and cogently argued throughout.

CHAPTER EIGHT: WHAT IS JUDAISM?

Cohen, Arthur A., and Paul Mendes-Flohr, eds. *Contemporary Jewish Religious Thought* (New York: The Free Press, 1987). A collection of essays on central Jewish philosophic topics by the greatest contemporary Jewish thinkers, this is a virtual encyclopedia of Jewish concepts. Each chapter is brief and intended for the layperson; it serves as an excellent way of beginning a process of study, either alone or with partners.

Hartman, David. *Conflicting Visions: Spiritual Possibilities of Modern Israel* (New York: Schocken Books, 1990). Though this book has not dealt in any length with the impact of Israel on modern spirituality, many Jews have their most powerful and spiritual Jewish moments in Israel. Hartman, one of Israel's most interesting philosophers, explores Israel's condition and some of its spiritual implications.

Telushkin, Joseph. *Jewish Literacy* (New York: William Morrow, 1991). This book is described in greater detail in the section on Chapter Two. It is an excellent volume for beginning a personal study of Jewish life. The brevity of each of its 346 chapters lends itself well to a person interested in reading a little bit each day. It also has good (though terse) bibliographic references throughout.

INDEX OF PRIMARY SOURCES

SUBJECT INDEX

---◇---

Daniel Gordis earned his doctorate at the School of Religion of the University of Southern California and was ordained as a rabbi at the Jewish Theological Seminary. He teaches at the University of Judaism in Los Angeles.

---◇---